W9-BMP-491

Women Speak

REFLECTIONS ON OUR STRUGGLES
1982 – 1997

Edited and compiled by
Shamim Meer

KWELA BOOKS
and OXFAM GB
in association with
SPEAK

Oxfam supported SPEAK as a funder in the 1980s.
Oxfam GB is associated with this book as co-publisher and distributor
in order to inform debate on issues of global equity and poverty reduction.
The views expressed are those of the contributors and editor,
not necessarily those of Oxfam GB.

Cover design by Karen Ahlschläger
Typography by Nazli Jacobs
Set in Times on DTP
Printed and bound by National Book Printers
Drukkery Street, Goodwood, Western Cape

First edition, first printing 1998

Kwela Books ISBN 0-7957-0082-2
Oxfam GB ISBN 0-85598-416-3

Contents

Foreword

In 1982 a group of women who were then members of the Durban Women's Group started SPEAK as a newsletter. We had a dream – of making sure that the struggles of our time would result in liberation for women too. Our newsletter was to be one vehicle for realising that dream.

In time the newsletter grew alongside the growing community, trade-union, and women's organisations of the 1980s to become a national magazine. Through its pages we were able to raise discussion and debate on issues of concern to women. And we gave support to the organising efforts of women. When distributing SPEAK through our visits to factories and through sales at rallies and meetings we continued the discussions and debates with readers, and we got important feedback which we brought into subsequent issues of the magazine.

We first thought of a book as a way of celebrating ten years of SPEAK in 1992. This book builds on the work started that year. However, the context we are in today – four years since our new government and since the closure of SPEAK – called for a different publication. We do see this book as a way of celebrating twelve years of SPEAK. In addition, the book looks back at past struggles from the perspective of the present in order to draw inspiration for present struggles that confront us.

Over the years the group of women working on SPEAK has changed and the SPEAK collective today includes two of the original founders. Working on SPEAK has been much more than a job for all of us. It has been a commitment and a way of life.

We thank all the women and men who contributed to SPEAK over the years. We thank all the writers whose work appears in this book. We thank Lesley Lawson, who began work on the manuscript which this book builds on. We thank all the funders who made our work possible through their support. In particular we would like to thank the Africa Groups of Sweden, the Africa Fund, the Canadian Embassy, the Catholic Fund for Overseas Development, the Communications Assistance Foundation, Christian Aid, CUSO, Development and Peace, the Fund for a Free South Africa, the Global Fund for Women, Grassroots International, the International Centre for Human Rights and Democratic Development, Interfund, Novib, Misereor, Oxfam UK, Oxfam Canada, SCAT, the South Coast Foundation, Trocaire and the World University Service.

SPEAK collective: Karen Hurt, Gill Lincoln, Libby Lloyd, Nise Malange, Shamim Meer, Jackie Mondi, Elinor Sisulu.

Introduction

Women have often been called mothers of the revolution but women were revolutionaries too. Women of all classes and races, women from urban and rural areas, women from all regions of South Africa played a significant role in the struggle against apartheid.

From the struggle's beginnings in the 1950s South African women fought alongside men in resisting apartheid. Women's militancy erupted at moments like 9 August 1956 when thousands of women from all over the country marched on the Government Offices in Pretoria to protest against passes for women. During the 1960s and 1970s when leaders and organisations were banned and exiled, many women suffered bannings, imprisonment and exile. Women made their voices heard within the liberation movement in exile. And as trade unions and community-based resistance against apartheid took off in the 1980s, women in these organisations spoke out on issues that affected their lives.

Women members of trade unions, community-based organisations and political organisations formed separate women's groups to organise women and to take up women's issues. From their small beginnings in local communities and factories these organisations grew during the 1980s, and in the 1990s they fed into the ANC Women's League and the Women's National Coalition, two organisations which made important gains for women during the negotiations and the run-up to the first democratic elections in the country.

Alongside the rise in political activity, the late 1970s also saw the beginnings of what came to be called the "alternative media". By the early 1980s these included the *South African Labour Bulletin, Work in Progress* and *Grassroots Community Newspaper*. These publications carried very little about women, however, and it was more often than not the voices of men that were heard in their articles.

SPEAK was started in 1983 by a group of women who were then working in different communities around housing struggles. We were also part of an initiative to set up a women's group, the Durban Women's Group. We started SPEAK as a newsletter for the group. But SPEAK was soon to grow into a national magazine alongside the other alternative publications.

We saw SPEAK as providing a space where black working-class women could speak out about the things that affected their lives. We felt very strongly that if women were to see liberation in a new South Africa we needed to organise and make sure that our demands were on the table. We wanted SPEAK to be a vehicle through which women could inspire other women as we struggled against the injustices of apartheid and worked to create a new South Africa.

The editorial of the first issue of SPEAK said:

SPEAK is a publication mainly for women. It deals with topics of interest to all people, we hope, but especially those which are useful and interesting to women. So, SPEAK is about women – their work in factories, homes and communities; their lives and problems, including their health, transport, housing, etc. Many of these problems apply to all people, but we are interested in the particular way they affect women, and the way in which women can and do respond to them. One way of raising these issues is through writing. We want this publication to reach women, and express their problems, thoughts and issues.

SPEAK was published from 1982 to the end of 1994. Women and men spoke out through its pages about women's position in society and about women's liberation. Women and men in trade unions, community organisations and political organisations read SPEAK and took part in discussions on crucial issues affecting women's lives.

This book brings together some of the voices of women on some of the critical issues of these times. The chapters cover key areas of struggle – communities, trade unions and politics, as well as crucial issues such as violence and personal struggles. The articles give a sense of what women were saying and doing during the 1980s and early 1990s up to the first year of the new government.

More recent interviews conducted in 1996 and 1997 include the voices of women on issues that face women in South Africa today. It is clear that in spite of the gains made in the new South Africa many of the struggles of the past continue to be struggles of the present. In addition there are new struggles confronting women today.

Among the victories women have won as a result of the years of struggle are the large number of women in Parliament, and the appointment of the Office of the Status of Women and the Commission for Gender Equality. The South African Constitution has a clause on gender equality. Various government departments are looking at ways of addressing gender equality within their work.

But despite the change in government and all the gains for women, the situation for the majority of women in South Africa has not changed much. The situation today is much the same as the situation described by South Africa's Minister of Health, Nkosazana Zuma, in her speech to the Beijing Conference in 1995:

Women in South Africa are definitely not free. The majority live in poverty and many cannot read or write. Millions do not have proper housing and no access to water, sanitation, education or health services. They are marginalised with no right to own land. Under customary law they marry and live lives as effective minors, subject to the authority of male relatives.

August 9 is South Africa's National Women's Day in commemoration of the march
by women against passes in 1956.   *Graphic: Shelly Sacks*

While we have seen political changes, these have not been matched by economic
improvements for women. While we have a clause in our constitution that guaran-
tees rights to women, the same constitution safeguards the rights of traditional leaders who perpetuate customary practices which tend to keep women as minors.

Women in various parts of the country continue to find ways to take up their
struggles within the new South Africa. These new struggles need new weapons.
Women need information, the means for effective lobbying, and more than ever be-

fore we need strong organisation. For without strong organisation representing the interests of black working-class women we will not see real changes for the majority of South African women. Yet women's organisations seem to have run out of steam just at the point when the challenges seem so much greater than before.

The situation today feels in some ways similar to the situation when SPEAK first started. Women in various communities were facing their problems, taking action and making headway. Yet much of this struggle was hidden. And there was no national or regional women's organisation bringing these isolated efforts together. We saw SPEAK's role as highlighting these local efforts and victories so as to inspire other women to organise and act. Today we have the need once more to know what women are doing and saying, so that we can draw support from each other in the new battles that face us.

Perhaps looking back at our past and listening to the voices of women from the pages of SPEAK will remind us of the struggles we have come from in order to go forward with greater strength. That is the purpose of this book.

The History of SPEAK

SPEAK was founded in 1982 by a group of women working in various communities in and around Durban. We were community activists addressing issues such as high rents. We decided to start a women's organisation – the Durban Women's Group – in order to ensure that women were actively involved in the struggles of the time. One of the sub-committees of the Durban's Women's Group was a newsletter sub-committee and this was to form the independent newsletter SPEAK.

The members of this sub-committee who were to become the founders of SPEAK included Sandy Africa, Monica Agulhas, Sheila Jalobe, Gugu Mji, Pregs Govender, Vanessa Taylor, Karen Hurt, Shamim Meer and Jane Quinn.

This was the time of emerging community organisations under the repressive conditions of apartheid. The period before this – the 1960s and 1970s – had been years of extreme repression in which organisations such as the ANC, the PAC and the SACP were banned and went into exile. Key men and women leaders had been banned or imprisoned. Political organisations in exile began the resistance that was to continue until the 1990s from outside South Africa's borders through both political and military pressure.

In the 1970s there was growing resistance from workers, beginning with the 1973 strikes in Durban, and from students within the Black Consciousness movement. The challenge to apartheid came to a peak in the Soweto uprising in 1976. Workers, students and communities within the country continued to organise resistance despite the costs of deaths, detentions, imprisonments and bannings.

The 1980s saw trade unions solidifying. As a result of pressure from capital and in response to the economic realities of the day, the government set up a commission on trade unions and took steps to legalise unions for African workers, a right previously denied them in law. Community struggles ensued with political activists playing a leading role in organising communities around issues such as rents and transport.

It was in this context that those of us who formed SPEAK came to organise women around community-based struggles. In our activism we attempted to link local community struggles with the struggle against the apartheid state. Our aim in setting up a women's group was to ensure women's rights within communities as well as within the broader struggle for a new post-apartheid South Africa.

The group included women from working-class African, coloured and Indian townships around Durban as well as students and professionals. Apartheid social engineering meant that each of the four race groups – Africans, coloureds, Indians and whites – were housed in separate "group areas". Resistance organisations, on the other hand, worked hard to bridge these imposed divides in order to unite workers, students and communities in opposition to the regime. Our women's group spent a lot of time bringing women from the various community groups together to share experiences and learn from each other – such things as how to start a pre-school, how to start a women's group and many other necessities. Because communities lived at considerable distances from each other, we had to overcome immense logistical hurdles of finding a centrally located venue, ensuring communication in a context where most working-class areas have no telephones, and arranging transport in the face of a virtually non-existent public transport system. Public transport was designed to get workers from home to work and back and did not cater for travel from one township to another or even from one section to another within a township. The middle-class women among us who had cars made these and themselves available in order to transport people, arranged venues, and acted as the contact persons between communities. All these tasks were reliant on voluntary activity.

After a few such meetings the idea of a newsletter hit us as an idea to be made a reality. We found that the exchanges among the women from various areas was invaluable. Women learnt from each other, inspired each other, found they were not alone in their problems, and often went back to put into action some new idea or another. Women wanted to share what they had learnt with other women in their townships (not more than one car load could make each meeting). A newsletter would enable such sharing to happen with a larger number of women, the printed form would enable people to reflect on and refer to articles when they needed to, and sharing could take place even when we were unable to organise face-to-face meetings.

With this as our inspiration we started work on the first issue of SPEAK. This inaugural issue was brought to a meeting of the women's group and put up on the wall for all to look at and comment. The cover article was on a recently held workshop of the women's group. Other articles included a report on a toy library organised by women in Tongaat South and one highlighting health problems.

We put out 200 copies of this newsletter in English and 200 in Zulu (the two spoken languages of the women in the group) and distributed them through the various women's groups. The response to the newsletter was positive beyond our expectations. There was much excitement and interest. The women in the group wanted more articles about the experiences of women in organising, and they wanted more on women's health.

SPEAK 2 called on women to write for SPEAK "about their experiences at home, in their communities and their jobs outside the home". It included articles on women organising in Chatsworth and in Clermont. SPEAK 3 had articles on women at a factory – Carnation Foods, on women in Northcroft in Phoenix township and on a bus boycott in Clermont. In all these articles we tried to record as faithfully as possible women's voices as they spoke to us about their lives. We wanted the publication to record women's voices. We wanted women to write and to learn how to produce a publication so that each community could have its own newsletter, and we saw SPEAK as a possible training ground to make this happen. While these training goals were not met, the newsletter SPEAK developed into the magazine which was to continue until 1994, which at its peak reached a distribution of 9 000, and which played a role in raising debate on issues of women's liberation within trade unions, community and political organisations, as well as in supporting and inspiring individual women in their daily struggles.

Early on a decision was made within the Durban Women's Group that the newsletter SPEAK should be independent from the women's group. This was a tactical decision, as it was felt that the magazine would have a longer lifespan if separated from the Women's Group, which was already under police scrutiny. At the time many community activists were being detained and police were watching all our meetings and tapping our telephones.

We saw SPEAK as a vehicle through which women could talk to other women so that they could be inspired to organise themselves and challenge various forms of oppression they experienced in the home, the community, the workplace and the country. We saw ourselves as community and trade-union activists. We distributed the magazine through our contacts in communities and trade unions, and we gathered articles by interviewing women and representing their voices as faithfully as possible in the pages of SPEAK. As organisation took off in all the parts of the country so too did our networks for distribution and article gathering.

As women's organisation in communities and trade unions grew throughout South Africa, women in other parts of the country saw SPEAK and became interested in the magazine. In about 1984 one of the collective members, and SPEAK's first staff person, Karen Hurt, travelled to Johannesburg with the magazine and got women in trade unions in particular interested in subscribing in bulk. Maggie Magubane, a trade unionist at the time and at present a member of the Gauteng Provincial Legislature, became one of our first bulk sellers around this time, continuing to sell SPEAK in her union until 1994.

Two SPEAK collective members sell magazines at the COSATU launch in 1985. *Photo: SPEAK*

Since we put out each issue of the magazine in English and Zulu, this in effect meant producing two magazines with each issue. Usually articles were written in English and then translated into Zulu. This was not without its problems, particularly since in the early years we had one Zulu-speaker on the collective. While articles in English went through several drafts in response to detailed comments from each of the collective members, articles in Zulu were translated by one translator and passed on the basis of the view of one SPEAK collective member. The quality of the Zulu magazine was therefore not equal to the English magazine.

When we started we all worked voluntarily. It was more than just another project. It was a political commitment. We met once a week in each others' homes – usually in the homes of those with the smallest children, who had no alternative child care. We worked on the design and layout on living-room floors and kitchen tables. We went out individually to interview women and wrote drafts which were then passed around for comment to each of the five or six collective members. Then we wrote up the final article after several rounds of passing copy around, so that by the end each article was truly a joint product. Initially we used our own resources and borrowed resources from other organisations. In time we were able to raise funds from overseas donors, including Oxfam Canada, Oxfam UK and I and Misereor. By 1985 we had opened an office and by 1986 we were able to employ our first staff persons – Karen Hurt and later that year Phumelele Ntombela and Jean Ngubane.

We did not have bylines in the early years. Nor did we identify collective mem-

15

bers. In part this was for security reasons (we were constantly under surveillance) but more because we believed in collective working and felt it was elitist to claim personal attention.

By 1988 we had opened a second office in Johannesburg and developed a large distribution network there. By then our major source of distribution was through trade-union contacts in factories and through sales at mass meetings and political rallies. There was an increasing demand for SPEAK and to our surprise we found that many men were reading the magazine too. We were at first both surprised and alarmed, for we had not thought of men as readers. But the more we thought about it, the more pleased we were, because we realised that it was important that we include men in discussion on women's rights. We began to include interviews with men – getting their views on matters such as violence against women, sharing housework, and abortion. Often our regular letter writers to the magazine were men. In addition to finding out about women's issues men also read the magazine because they felt it gave them information on the struggles of the times in a clear, accessible manner.

We were sometimes challenged by male readers with comments such as the "beating of women by men should be left in the bedroom". We challenged them back and were able to open and stimulate discussion on important areas of women's lives that were often not spoken about in public. And when women in trade unions were battling to get issues such as sexual harassment in the unions on the table for discussion we were able to support them by writing about it in the pages of SPEAK.

COSATU women send a message with SPEAK posters at a rally to protest the Labour Relations Amendment Act in 1990.   *Photo: SPEAK*

Significant points in SPEAK's life were an evaluation conducted in 1989 and a marketing survey in 1991. Following recommendations from the 1989 evaluation we decided to change the collective structure to a managing committee and to stop the Zulu publication. These decisions were in the interests of greater efficiency and were made on the basis that the demand for the Zulu SPEAK had dropped while the demand for the English SPEAK was on the increase. Following the 1991 marketing survey, and in response to the changing political climate after the reforms of 1990/1991, we decided to enter a distribution agreement with a national newspaper and magazine distributor in order to reach larger numbers. Our previous distribution was done by staff who would visit factories and communities to drop off magazines and collect money from sales. We also had a network of sellers and often during the 1980s they would be harassed by police for selling SPEAK and other alternative publications.

The political reforms opened the opportunity for the first time of considering distribution via a magazine distributor. However, going this route meant producing SPEAK monthly, going glossy and increasing the number of pages per magazine. We took on this challenge from mid-1992. We were able to raise the funds to employ more staff and managed from 1992 to the end of 1994 to produce a monthly magazine. Reaching a larger audience meant that in addition to articles for our traditional readership – who were members of women's, community and trade-union groupings – we were trying to reach individuals outside of organisations. The appeal of the magazine had to be broadened.

The changing political times are reflected in the content of SPEAK from 1992 onwards. The unbannings of key political organisations and the move towards negotiations on the country's future brought new issues of debate and a greater focus on national issues. SPEAK played a role in providing information and a platform for debate on women's role within the negotiations and women's place in the new South Africa. During 1993 a strong focus was placed on voter education since this was the first opportunity for the majority of South Africans to participate in democratic elections.

In 1992 SPEAK branched out into radio, with the establishment of a radio project aimed at providing training to community groups and at producing audio tapes for distribution to emerging community radio stations. The radio project provided training to rural women in Moutse in the rural Northern Transvaal, who set up a community radio station. And we worked with Radio Zibonele in the Western Cape, helping to put it on the air.

SPEAK magazines in 1994 document some of the key issues during that historic year of the election and the formation of the first democratically elected government. By the middle of 1994, however, SPEAK had lost a significant number of its skilled staff and the search for replacements was proving impossible. New opportunities had opened up for media activists both within government and within radio and television. Within this climate it was difficult for SPEAK to retain or attract the few women media activists in the country. By the end of 1994 we had to make the difficult and painful decisions to close both SPEAK magazine and SPEAK Radio.

Earlier in 1994 we had seen the closure of *Work in Progress* and *Learn and Teach*, two other alternative publications, as a result of the withdrawal of funders from South Africa following the end of apartheid. Today the alternative media is sorely missed in a context in which the print media are increasingly in the hands of monopolies.

SPEAK continues today as a project putting out occasional publications and working on a video project. We hope to continue making some small contribution to push the struggle for women's rights a little further along.

Organisation of the Book

Each chapter of this collection covers what we see as key areas of women's struggles. Chapters begin with a brief introduction, followed by articles from the pages of SPEAK and more recent interviews which reflect struggles today. Each chapter ends with a poem.

In chapters one and two, women in communities and trade unions highlight the key issues raised in SPEAK over the years, as well as the attempts by women to deal with their immediate problems. In addition, interviews conducted in 1996 and 1997 reflect some of the concerns of women since the historic 1994 elections.

Women speak on the fight against violence against women in chapter three. At present, violence against women is seemingly on the increase and far more in the public eye than ever before. This is one area in which women have now come together nationally – in a network against violence against women.

Chapter four concerns women's fight against what are seen as "personal" problems, but which have much to do with the distribution of power in society, confirming the link between the personal and the political.

In the fifth chapter, women (and one man) from political organisations at the forefront of the struggle speak about women's liberation during the years of resistance against apartheid.

In the final chapter, women speak about their role in negotiations and in parliament. This chapter also raises the issue of an autonomous women's organisation as an appropriate forum for addressing women's liberation, and a more current interview relates the attempts of women in the Western Cape to set up such an organisation.

Significant themes from the pages of SPEAK which are not included in this collection include women's health (every issue from the magazine's inception had a health focus), AIDS, young women, women and culture, and interviews with men on their views on women's liberation. Nevertheless, the articles that follow give a representative sample of some of the main issues dealt with in the magazine.

We hope the selection of articles will serve to celebrate women's lives and contributions as well as provide inspiration for current struggles.

CHAPTER ONE

Women in Communities

When we started SPEAK in 1982, we (the founders of SPEAK) were ourselves working in various black (that is African, coloured and Indian) working-class communities in and around Durban. We worked with strong women who were organising around their immediate needs as well as taking up their rights against repressive local authorities and the apartheid state. These actions were "hidden" within each local area, and were given little coverage in any branches of the media, including the alternative media. We started the newsletter that was to become SPEAK magazine in order to highlight these "hidden" achievements and struggles. We hoped this would inspire women in all parts of South Africa to organise and act so that women's liberation would be part of our national liberation. We try in this chapter to capture some of the key issues for women in communities over the years through a selection of articles from SPEAK magazine.

Women speak in these articles about their work to organise and deal with their problems. This was an era when nothing good was expected from the government. Where if anything the government's agenda was to create greater hardship for black South Africans. Women realised that they had to find ways of coping in order to meet their basic needs even as they confronted the authorities.

The articles are arranged in three sub-themes: women organising in local communities, the Rural Women's Movement, and women and political violence in communities.

The first subject was well documented in SPEAK. Women speak about their work in organising a women's group and pre-schools. About a campaign against high rents and evictions at a time when police had camped on hills overlooking their township and went on the rampage, firing teargas and beating and raping township residents. Women tell how they took up the issues of a burial ground and a dump site with the local authority. A woman tells of the clinic she built and runs in her yard. Women talk of how they support each other on problems of sexual abuse and violence against them.

The Rural Women's Movement, the second sub-theme of this chapter, was formed in 1991. This movement took up local struggles and played an important part in pushing the demands of rural women during the negotiations leading up to the election. In the articles in this chapter, women from the Rural Women's Movement speak out about their struggles for land, water and health care. They speak also of their struggle for a place for women in the traditional authority structures.

The struggle for land and authority was a significant struggle in the years before 1994. At the 1994 Community Land Conference, held a few months before South Africa's first democratic elections, Ellen Ntsoelengoe of the Rural Women's Movement said: "Not only do we have to deal with the fact that the government gave most of the land to whites, but also with traditional leaders and men in our community who do not want women to own the little land that is left." The Rural Women's Movement continues to organise around these and other issues today.

Political violence is the final sub-theme of this chapter. In many parts of the country women were the ones who had to deal with the violence sweeping through their communities. In articles in this chapter, women from KwaZulu-Natal speak in 1987 of their experiences in the war created by men. Women in Umlazi, also in KwaZulu-Natal, describe their march to get police out of the township in 1990. Women from Boipatong in the Vaal give an account of their march, a year later, demanding an end to the killings in their area. Women from the East Rand speak in 1994 of their march to the ANC offices, calling for action to end the violence they experience daily.

Today these acts of violence are fewer. In some parts of KwaZulu-Natal, however, violence continues to wreak havoc on community lives. And more generally, the years of violence have led to a culture of violence that we see in the high crime rate and the increasing number of rapes on women.

FROM THE PAGES OF *SPEAK*

Women Organise in their Local Communities

In the following articles women from various communities tell of their struggles and attempts to organise around local issues. Women have always organised to survive, to make ends meet and to challenge their oppression. These struggles and challenges hardly ever make news. SPEAK wanted to show these everyday struggles and challenges in order to acknowledge them and to celebrate what women were doing, so that other women would be inspired.

SPEAK 3, 1983
Northcroft women organise

"Northcroft, Unit 14 is a new area in Phoenix township. We had been living here for about a year when members of the Phoenix Women's Circle and Phoenix Child Welfare visited two women in the area. They told us about the Phoenix Women's Circle and asked us if we would like to start women's groups. They discussed people's needs such as créches, child care and pre-schools."

The Northcroft women agreed to invite other women from their area to get more views and more support for the idea of setting up a women's group. A meeting was held at one of the women's homes. She invited her neighbour and a few other women she knew. There were about ten people at the meeting.

At the first meeting we chose handwork and pre-schools as areas for action. It was agreed that we would ask the school principal if she would allow us to use classrooms after school for this. To get more women involved we decided to have meetings on each street, and to go door to door to invite women to the meetings. Visiting each home was an interesting experience. Most women were very interested. We held street meetings covering more than 500 houses. Many women attended these meetings. Many of us did not know women in the neighbourhood before, so this gave us a chance to meet each other. At each meeting someone offered her home for the next meeting.

Women agreed that we should start a pre-school. Two women volunteered to teach at the pre-school. The school principal agreed we could use classrooms every afternoon from 12.30 to 2.30.

We also spoke of transport problems and of the problem of no clinic. We started handwork groups in each street. Women met once a week to teach and learn crocheting, knitting and baking.

We organised a big meeting for the whole area. The women from the street groups went to every house, inviting women to the big meeting. The meeting was held at the football ground as there is no hall in our area. About 60 women attended this meeting. It was a very windy day and the water sprinkler made some of us a little wet! We also had to shout to hear each other. But the meeting went on and everyone agreed we should have one women's group. After this big meeting we called a meeting of two people from each street to work on a constitution for the group. We have passed the constitution and we have a working committee that meets once a month. Our pre-school is now running and we have had two cake sales, a jumble sale and a variety show to raise funds.

We have got a lot out of the group. But at times very few people come to meetings. We are working very hard and we feel each member has a part to play in building a strong group. We feel everyone must have a say and that our officials alone can't make decisions. This is why our meetings are important. So that we can discuss things and have our say before we decide anything.

As women we must go forward

The Lamontville Women's Group, formed in November 1983, is a branch of the Natal Organisation of Women (NOW). NOW is a new organisation in Natal.

"Things had been very bad in Lamontville in 1983. There was fighting in Lamontville after Mr Dube was killed. Mr Dube was a popular leader in Lamontville. He fought against rent increases. He showed how badly the administration board was dealing with house repairs, and how the community councillors did not represent the community. His killing was an injury against the community because he supported the struggles of the community.

"After Mr Dube was killed police came in with teargas. They drove around Lamontville shooting teargas. They came into the houses shooting teargas. Police camped in the hills for a whole month. They would come into the houses, kicking doors and hitting people with sjamboks. One of the members of our group came home one night and there was blood all over the house. The police had hit her son. Women were raped by police. It was really bad."

The women's group spoke about these and other problems, such as rent and transport increases. In March they decided to see the superintendent of Lamontville as he was threatening to evict people who could not pay. They believed as women "we would be safe from teargas and shooting". The woman were able to get a meeting with the superintendent. "We asked him why the rents were going up when the houses were cracked and broken."

We are a force to reckon with – Hambanati Women's Action Group

Women together are strong! There is no other way to describe the women's group of Hambanati. A man from Hambanati had told us: "Hambanati is a place with a difference – the women dominate organisation there!"

Hambanati women told us: "We had lots of problems. In 1979 our cemetery was full and we were told to bury our dead at Ntuzuma, very far away, or to cremate our dead which we did not want to do."

The women decided to organise a meeting. "We went house to house and demanded of all women to come to a meeting to talk about this problem. Anyone refusing to come had to tell us where she hoped to bury her dead. Did she have a special place, we asked.

"We met with the advisory board but found they had no power to do anything. We formed the Hambanati Women's Action Group and took up the problem with the Port Natal Administration Board."

The group got a burial ground closer-by at Gennezana. "But there was a jump in cost from R12 to R53." The women fought this and got the cost lowered to R12.

Another problem they took up was the problem of the dump site near their township. "Lots of flies, smells, dirty water and papers got into our yards from the nearby dump site. We said we would block the rubbish trucks from entering the township and if they went on dumping we would take the rubbish and dump it on their beautiful golf course in Tongaat! They soon opened a new dump site and cleaned our place. Now that our organisation is solid the Port Natal Administration Board know we are a force to be reckoned with."

SPEAK 14, 1987
Working and sharing together

St Wendolins is a place outside Marianhill in Natal. There is green grass and banana and mango trees around the houses. But some old houses stand empty. These are the houses of people who left the area when the government threatened to uproot and remove the community. SPEAK was here to talk to the St Wendolins women who work together on vegetable gardens. It was a rainy day but we managed to talk to some women as we ran from one garden to another between the showers of rain.

"We plant our vegetables to eat at home and to sell." The land is owned by the Marianhill Institute and the women have use of the land at no charge. Six to eight women share a plot and work together. They share seeds and they share the job of selling. "We trust each other. We know each other's plots. We sell for each other. If someone comes looking for cabbage, I know who has it ready, then I sell it for her if she is not around. She will then get the money from me when we see each other."

The women have also started sewing classes together. "What I earn from selling vegetables and what I sew contributes towards school fees and buying my children's clothes. My husband is very happy that we share the financial load."

Coming together like this is not something new in St Wendolins. For many years the government wanted to uproot the community, and the community resisted this and won. Organising together and sharing together is part of building the future we look forward to – when we have a government that cares about the people in the country and when we have a new system where all people have an equal chance to a decent, happy life.

SPEAK 21, 1988
Eldorado Park Women's Group organise child care

The Eldorado Park Women's Group runs a child care project. Mallie Fakir told us how this started: "One woman decided to get a women's group together. She called meetings but only five women came each time. We decided not to wait for others. People were not interested in meetings. If there was something concrete, people would be more interested. So the five of us started small to show people what we could do."

They decided to start a child care project as there were no pre-schools and children were playing in the streets. Mallie had taught small children for eighteen years and she brought ideas to the group. Three members of the group were willing to teach.

SPEAK

St. Wendolins Women Working and Sharing Together

Eldorado Park Women's Group Child Care Project, July 1988 – preparing children for the new South Africa.
Photo: Gille, You and Me Images

The women approached the Muslim Council for use of classrooms next to the mosque. The women borrowed money from friends. One husband gave a part of his salary to the group every month.

The group started their first classes. But it was not easy. Teachers did not get paid every month. Some parents were able to pay for their children, others could not. When the women found that many children were coming hungry to school they began preparing sandwiches for them. The group also took up the housing problems of families who were moved into a tent settlement in Eldorado Park. The group works closely with other organisations in the area, like the Progressive Teachers' Union, the Advice Centre, and youth group and housing committees.

The care groups have grown and are run in two homes while families are away at work. The women see their work as preparing children for the new South Africa. They want the children to learn to respect themselves. To share with each other. And to see all people as equal. They have made their own stories and songs for the children, since very few stories in books are about working-class or black children. And very few show women and girls as strong people.

The Eldorado Park Women's Group has joined the Federation of Transvaal Women (FEDTRAW), an organisation that brings together women from different areas to fight for their rights as people, workers and women.

We spoke to Mallie Fakir more recently about her work in 1996 with the Women's Institute for Leadership, Democracy and Development. The interview is at the end of this chapter.

SPEAK 36, 1991

A clinic in a yard *by Bobby Rodwell*

When Mary Agnes spoke to people in her community about her plan to open a maternity clinic for women, they said: "This one must be dreaming." Takalani clinic in Khuma township in the Western Transvaal stands today as proof of her ability to make her dream come true. Takalani means joy.

The clinic was built in Mary Agnes' yard. A double garage and two small rooms have been turned into a bright and sunny clinic. There are seven beds in two wards with cribs for babies, a delivery room, an examination room and a place where patients wait to be seen.

Takalani has two trained nurses, Mary Agnes and her sister Martha Khunoana. There are also five trainee nurses. The clinic is open 24 hours a day. In the one month since the clinic opened, four women have given birth here and 28 patients have been seen.

Kuma township is in a mining area. When the influx control laws were scrapped in 1986, women could join their husbands or boyfriends there. This led to a growing need for decent maternity services. But there were none to be found. Mary Agnes said: "Many women had babies at home. These home births often resulted in death, either of the baby or both the mother and child. We heard many such stories and I saw it myself.

"The final blow came when the Tsepong Hospital refused to treat patients from out of town. An important inspiration for me was Eva Modise, who operated a clinic from her four-room house in Soweto. Her family lived in three small rooms and the fourth one was turned into a clinic. She did this even though her husband was in exile and times were hard."

When Mary Agnes tried to raise money she found no one would take her seriously, so she started saving her own money. After a few years she was ready to make a start. She got some support from local businessmen, but she paid most costs out of her own money. She decided to start the clinic and then try to find funding.

Mary Agnes spoke proudly of her clinic. She gave up a secure job as professional nurse at the Vaal Reefs Hospital and risked all her money to open Takalani. Why? "It's simple," said Mary Agnes. "There was a need and I could help. I am a nurse and what's more I am trained as a community nurse. How could I ignore the needs of women in my own community?"

Mary Agnes believes women should push ahead strongly to achieve a better life. She said: "Women should know how strong they are and try by all means to achieve their dreams. We must all work together and we can start to make a better life for women in South Africa."

SPEAK 47, 1993

Together we are strong by *Mahadi Miya*

Land ownership, sexual abuse, theft, legal disputes … these are some of the issues women in Tamboville and Wattville are organised around. The SPEAK team went to investigate.

It was a cold night. By seven o'clock the air was dark and full of the smoke of coal stoves. More than 150 women were gathering in a church hall in Wattville township, many of them huddled in blankets. They had come with a purpose. Once every two weeks women from Tamboville and Wattville meet to share and solve problems through their Women's Forum. This was one of their meetings.

Kgomotso Rammego, the chairperson of the forum, told SPEAK that forming the forum was the idea of women in the Wattville Civic Association. "We work hand in hand with the civic by referring some cases to it, like the problems of allocation of stands," said Rammego.

The women decided to have a separate forum because they wanted to discuss their problems privately. Women were not able to talk about some painful and personal issues in front of the men in the civic. Rammego explains: "Women find it easier to talk freely amongst other women in the forum. They know that other women will understand their problems and give them the support they need. Also, privacy is one of the main rules of the forum."

There was also a need for a forum in which all women could take part – women from different political organisations as well as women who were not politically active.

"Our forum was formed firstly to help women who were being beaten by their boyfriends and husbands," said Rammego. "Secondly, we wanted to stop the men taking over women's stands and houses. A typical case is that of the woman who manages to get a stand for herself. Her boyfriend helps her by providing the building material for the shack. After the shack is built, the couple starts having problems. Then the boyfriend kicks the woman out and brings another girlfriend."

At the meeting tonight, sexual abuse was one of the main issues discussed. You could feel the anger in the air. One woman told of a 60-year-old man who had sexually abused a four-year-old child. The child was examined by the district surgeon and another doctor. The woman was worried because the police had taken the doctor's certificate and now three months later they had done nothing about the case. She wondered if the evidence had been destroyed.

The issue was discussed for a long time. The chairperson said angrily, "The police handling the case are black. They may have children of their own who are also in trouble – why don't they do something about it?" The forum agreed that Rammego would follow up the case. She would get a copy of the doctor's certificate and a list of the names of the people involved.

Child abuse is causing a lot of pain in this community. In many cases children are abused by members of their own family or close relatives. Women say they will no longer keep quiet about this.

One woman said, "Most of us keep quiet because we think we are protecting our families. The truth is we are actually killing the child by not getting this problem solved."

A mother said she had found her daughter sleeping with her husband, the girl's stepfather. She wanted advice. "It depends on you," she was told. "You have to decide whether you want to stay with that kind of husband. We would not like to be accused of breaking or destroying your marriage and your home. If you want to take legal action you will have to be prepared to stand in court with your husband and accuse him of abusing your child. This will be difficult if you still want to stay married to this man."

The women talked about the difficulty of bringing up children in townships. They are worried about sexual activity among young children. An example was given of a two-year-old girl and a four-year-old boy found having sex.

One woman said, "This is caused by the lack of privacy in our homes. We stay in small shacks. We are forced to share a tiny sleeping area with our children. I blame this problem on the lack of proper housing."

At the meeting mothers were advised, "Make time for your children and encourage an open relationship. Do not be embarrassed to discuss certain things with your children. Answer their questions honestly. Do not think that by ignoring the problem it will go away."

Another case that was raised was one of a six-year-old drinking at shebeens and demanding liquor from her parents. The chairperson got the names and addresses of the child and the shebeens where she drinks. Someone commented, "Alcohol abuse is encouraged by parents who give beer to babies and children. Children easily become addicted to beer."

Apart from arranging for counselling, the forum arranges for legal advice for those who cannot afford it. It also puts people in contact with organisations which can help with their particular problem. Rammego also encourages other women to start these kinds of groups.

Women face many painful problems – in their relationships with men, in bringing up children and within their communities. Tamboville and Wattville women show us that when we organise together, such problems are more easily solved.

SPEAK 65, 1994
Radio with a difference by Gail Reagon

Community radio stations are springing up everywhere. But Radio Zibonele in Khayelitsha is different – it is run mainly by women.

Except for the big aerial and the truck outside, the Zibonele Health Project looks like any other house in the crowded and dusty Griffiths Extension in Khayelitsha, Cape Town. But for the past three years, this building has been a community health clinic serving about 20 000 people who live in Griffith and the surrounding areas.

And in the past eighteen months, the Zibonele Health Project has become more than just a health centre. The project now houses one of the most successful community radio stations in the country – Radio Zibonele. The radio station was born from the vision of community health care. The aim was that it should focus on education about how to prevent illness.

The project employs fifteen people, most of them women. Each one does at least 125 home visits a month to educate and inform people about health issues. "With radio," said Miriam Hlazo, "we are able to do a lot more education work around health. We can reach more people."

"Members of the community also use the radio to broadcast messages about meetings and community events," added Portia Ngondeka.

The setting up of the station was supported by the National Progressive Primary Health Care Network's Media Training Centre. Initially, four women health workers were trained by Bush Radio in Cape Town. They still attend regular training sessions to improve their broadcasting skills. "Each and every health worker at the project participates in Radio Zibonele," said Thandi Zabungcu.

Besides dealing with health issues, Radio Zibonele offers advice and covers social issues ranging from how to raise funds to advertising community meetings. "The only area we did not cover was politics," said Ngondeka.

All programmes are broadcast in Xhosa, the local language.

Radio Zibonele is an example of people taking control of their lives. Through the health and radio projects the people of Khayelitsha, especially women, have been empowered.

"We used to broadcast every Tuesday, from 9 a.m. to 11.40 a.m. but stopped at the end of March because we did not have a license," Radio Zibonele's Snowy Mocha explains. "We applied for a temporary broadcasting license and the community signed a petition in support of our application."

When Radio Zibonele suspended its operations in March it was already a well-established community radio station. The station's application for a license has received a lot of support. In July three members of the Independent Broadcasting Authority (IBA) visited Zibonele and "were very impressed with what we are doing," said Mocha proudly. The IBA is a body which issues radio licenses to community and other radio stations. "We told them we needed a permanent license because we want to broadcast every day from 9 a.m. to 4 p.m. We want to develop our community. They promised us that we would know by the end of August."

But like their name, Zibonele – "we see for ourselves" – these are not people who sit around waiting for things to happen. At the time of the interview they were busy working on programmes which will go on air as soon as the license is issued.

And, because community involvement does not stop with adults, Radio Zibonele is teaching children how to broadcast. Three months ago the "Child to Child" project was launched. Children aged between six and fourteen years were trained in broadcasting during a week-long workshop run by staff members, SPEAK's Radio Audio

Programme (RAP) executive producer Libby Lloyd and Dr Gabriel Urgoiti from the Media Training Centre. "The children were great. They kept on saying, we want to make an interview. We want to make our own songs," Mocha said. Programmes produced by the children were recorded and will be broadcast to the community as soon as Radio Zibonele gets its license.

Radio Zibonele is the envy of many communities. And so are the people who run it. Mocha, Hlazo, Ngondeka and Zabungcu – young independent mothers, health workers and radio presenters and producers – are proud to be part of this community effort. Among them they have seven children. Three are single parents. All of them are community health workers. It is even more encouraging that the community supports the project. "Before we thought we couldn't do anything without men. Now that we are in this great project, we are powerful and the community encourages us," said Zabungcu.

Rural Women's Movement

A major movement among community women was the Rural Women's Movement, formed in 1992. This organisation was responsible for ensuring that rural women's voices were heard during the national negotiations and in the drafting of the country's constitution.

Rural Women's Movement members celebrate the launch of their organisation in November 1991.

Photo: Gille, You and Me Images

SPEAK 38, 1992

Rural women's voices ring out *by Libby Lloyd*

In November 1991, 120 women from rural areas in the Transvaal and northern Orange Free State launched the Transvaal Rural Women's Movement at the Lobethal Mission in Lebowa.

They came from Huhudi, from Marapong, Oukasie, Driefontein, Ga-Maphopha – from 28 rural communities. They came with a common aim – "to create forums for rural women to unite against oppression".

According to the constitution, the Transvaal Rural Women's Movement is "open to all oppressed rural women who wish to join our struggle for women's rights". They came together because of a "shared history of suffering because of apartheid, land policies, forced removals and incorporation". The women also share a history of fighting hard to end suffering. They fought for their right to live on their ancestors' land and to look after that land. They are still fighting for the right to water, health clinics, education and the right to have a say in their communities.

Communities in the western and south-eastern Transvaal came up with the idea of the Rural Women's Movement in May 1990. The Transvaal Rural Action Committee (TRAC) helped organise meetings in other communities and slowly the movement grew. The women talked about forced removals, about the problems they face in their own communities where men are treated as kings. They talked about the need to build a strong organisation for rural women.

The women are determined their organisation will not be just a talkshop. They are teaching each other skills in gardening, basket-making, and dress-making. They have many plans. "We must demand that women have equal rights to land. Women should have a say in political matters in our communities." This is a burning issue as women are not allowed to go to the decision-making body in their community, the kgotla. Their husbands, brothers or fathers speak for them. The women are determined to fight for their right to have a say.

"We are living in new times," says one woman. "In the past women were not even allowed to sit on chairs in the presence of men. Women take care of the most important things in life – health, education and the family – and should be represented at all levels in society from the kgotla to parliament."

The women feel strongly that the organisation must give rural women a voice in the new South Africa. "The executive must make sure our voices are heard or we will be left out. They must be the ears and eyes for us about discussions on women's issues around the country."

SPEAK 45, 1992
WE WANT WATER! – Moutse women on the march
by Thoraya Pandy

Women from Moutse in the northern Transvaal marched to demand an end to "water apartheid".

Moutse is just two hours' drive from the fountains and swimming pools of Johannesburg. But in this rural dust bowl, black people struggle for every precious drop of water.

The Moutse municipality says it does not have money to provide underground water pipes because Moutse is such a large area and the 42 villages of Moutse are too far away from each other.

The Moutse community says this is nonsense. "The Loskop Dam supplies water to white farmers who live right next to us. It also supplies water to Lebowakgomo, which is much further," said Ntwane Podile, a Moutse resident. While white farmers have irrigation pipes to water their crops, there are very few taps in Moutse. People get water from wells, boreholes and rivers – many of which are drying up because of the drought. "We have to get up at four o'clock in the morning and walk very far to fetch water from a river," said Mokgetjsane Ramadumetjsa. "The water from the river is not always clean, but we are forced to drink it and use it," she added.

Martha Motlamoyane says Moutse people have to use the same water over and over again to "wash our bodies, to water our plants and give to the animals. We don't throw water away once it has been used, even if it is dirty."

Sometimes government trucks supply water to the villages. It costs as much as R2,50 for 200 litres. When these trucks do not come, families go without water.

The water situation in Moutse became so bad in October 1992 that the Rural Women's Movement organised a protest march. More than a thousand people, mainly women, marched from Tambo Square Stadium to the offices of the Transvaal Provincial Administration, where they handed over their demands. The six kilometre march took more than two hours in the hot, blazing sun.

Martha Motlamoyane said: "Women and men came from all over Moutse to join in this march. Some left their homes even before the sun was up, to be here. The drought has really united the people." Mokgetjsane Ramadumetjsa said: "We are marching because for three years we have been asking for water taps and electricity for all the villages."

Motlamoyane told SPEAK why women were so active in the water protests: "Women live here in the rural areas while men work in the cities. We are the ones who have to look after the children, the land, animals and everything else."

Mama Lydia Kompe – a member of the Rural Women's Movement – who led the march, told SPEAK why the drought is especially hard for women. "Pregnant women do not have water, milk and fresh vegetables. How can you feed a baby if there is not enough drinking water? The education of the children is also seriously affected because they have to get up at four in the morning to fetch water," she said. "When they get into the classroom they fall asleep. And they cannot even get a drink of water at school, because there are no taps."

Women from Moutse demand an end to "water apartheid" – September 1992.

Photo: Elmond Jiyane, CDC Photo Unit

Water shortages also cause arguments between people who wait at the water points. "Sometimes people wait for hours, and when they get to the water hole, it's dry," said Kompe.

Kompe believes that the drought is causing a lot of stress among women. "They are worried about their lives, and they worry if next year will be as bad as 1992."

SPEAK 60, 1994

This is our land *by Rosalee Telela*

The Community Land Conference was the first-ever gathering of rural and landless people to voice their demands about land. Ellen Ntsoelengoe knows the suffering caused by forced removals. In 1990 she joined the Rural Women's Movement to do something about this. "The majority living in rural areas are black women who have no jobs, no land, and very little formal education. Not only do we have to deal with the fact that the government gave most of the land to whites, but also with traditional leaders and men in our community who do not want women to own the little land that is left," she explained. "If women could own land on their own they would be able to survive on their own and not depend on men."

Yvonne Padi form Modderfontein said traditional laws and practices make it difficult for women to have control over land. "Only men have the right to own land and only sons can inherit land. A woman living in a rural area and who is in a customary marriage

33

is like a child with no rights. She has no say in what goes on." Padi says life became more difficult for women after the land was taken away from black people. "Men go to towns to work while women are left to care for the children, the land and the animals."

Through organisation and mobilisation women are fighting, not only for land but for control over their lives. This is what the Rural Women's Movement has been doing, says Padi. "Where I live it is not like before when the chiefs, kgotlas or the government told us what to do. Women no longer accept things until they have met and discussed things."

Already women have made some important strides through organising. The constitution for the new South Africa says men and women are equal and there must be no discrimination against women. During the negotiations, traditional leaders demanded that customary and traditional law should be more important than the constitutional principal of equality between men and women. Women, including the Rural Women's Movement, fought this and won their battle. "As a result, it will now be possible for women to own land. This victory is a result of women's groups growing and the acceptance that it is time women started learning to take the future in their own hands," Ntsoelengoe said.

Ntsoelengoe and Padi want the new government to address the demands of rural women in a serious way. "They should train women so that they can stand on their own and also lead the nation. They must make sure women are educated because there are thousands of women who never went to school. Many do not know how to vote because they cannot read and write. There has to be political education for women because often women do not know what is going on. They have to close not only the gap between races but also the gap between men and women which has been open for so long.

"As women we have to build ourselves and show those women who are not interested that we will fight for what women need."

SPEAK 63, 1994

Moutse's battle for health care by *Rosalee Telela*

The people and women of Moutse in the Eastern Transvaal have a long history of resistance. This 700 000-strong community resisted being part of KwaNdebele. They also fought for land, water, schools, clinics and better education. Faced with lack of health services they are now determined to fight this.

"There is only one hospital, called Philadelphia, which has 600 beds and serves the 1,4 million people of Moutse and KwaNdebele. There are only two clinics and some mobile units which visit once a month," said Martha Matlala, chairperson of the newly formed Moutse Health Forum. "There is a shortage of beds, food, medicine and doctors."

The women of Moutse wrote to the former health minister (in the National Party government) Dr Rina Venter. Matlala said, "We met with her but nothing concrete came of the meeting. Later we met with people from the national health department and the Philadelphia hospital board. The civics were part of the negotiating team. We made our demands as women and rural people."

The Moutse Health Forum consists of the Rural Women's Movement, the National Education and Health Workers' Union, Moutse Civic, the Congress of Traditional Leaders of South Africa, the Youth Development Forum and local health committees.

The Health Forum has demanded that half the hospital board includes elected community representatives – and won. "Our membership on the board will be useful only if we unite," said Matlala. There are plans to train community health workers who will be based in communities "so women will not have to walk long distances with babies on their backs". By focusing on prevention of illnesses, the costs of health services and transport will be reduced.

Matlala told us, "When women are empowered to deal with their own health they can participate more actively in the social, political and economic life of the community." Adequate water supply plays an important part in a community's well-being. "You cannot expect people to be in good health if they do not have a supply of clean water. Women, even those pregnant and old, have to walk long distances to fetch water. It is women and children who suffer most when the health care system is bad."

Women and Political Violence in Communities

In the mid-1980s violence tore apart communities in Natal. By the late-1980s parts of the Transvaal were also up in flames. Women speak in these articles of their experiences in these wars that were not of their making but which made their lives close to impossible.

SPEAK 22, 1988
We are dying my child

"I heard a big bang at the door. I jumped out of bed. It was midnight. There was shouting and swearing outside. Men demanded that I open the door. They wanted R10 for joining Inkatha. I did not have that R10. I thought, 'God, now its my turn to die.'" This is how one woman from Harewood, near Pietermaritzburg, described an attack on her house.

"It was just me and my three children inside. My eldest son was at college. I was scared, but my children were brave. They did not cry, although they knew they could die at any time. I didn't open the door and after a lot of swearing the men left. At 4 a.m. I took my children and ran to a relative's house. Two hours later I saw a cloud of smoke. It was my house. It burned to ashes with all I had inside. A month later the police shot and killed my eldest son. They said he had a dangerous weapon. I demanded that the police show me the weapon, but they could not."

By 1988 Natal had become a war zone – women support each other at a funeral at Mpophomeni near Pietermaritzburg.   *Photo: Cedric Nunn*

The fighting in Natal has affected many thousands of people. The fighting has turned Natal into a war zone. In 1988 more than one thousand people were killed in the Pietermaritzburg area. Many women have been raped. And more than 7 000 people are homeless.

Some say that the fighting is between Inkatha on the one hand, and the United Democratic Front (UDF) and the Congress of South African Trade Unions (COSATU) on the other. Others say it is black-on-black violence. There is also another side – many say that the police and the government are sympathetic to Inkatha. Since the fighting started, many people from the UDF and COSATU have been detained or restricted. But Inkatha is not restricted. It is given time on the radio and the television to promote itself.

SPEAK travelled to Ashdown, a township outside Pietermaritzburg, to meet women who live in the war zone. We wanted to know how they were coping.

"Siyafa wemntanami. We are dying my child," said one woman. "This hard life started two years ago. This whole area was very quiet until people were forced to join Inkatha. If you do not want to be an Inkatha member they say you are a UDF member. Then you could be killed."

It is not only UDF members who get killed. It is often their whole family. A priest in the area told us: "On the second floor of the Edenvale hospital there is a little girl. Her home was attacked in the middle of the night. They shot and killed her sister and

36

mother, shot and wounded her father. She was shot through the back of the neck and is paralysed. She is only seven years old. She does not understand the politics of Inkatha or UDF."

The war has affected the lives of women in particular ways. Most women had never worked outside the home before. Now that they have lost husbands and sons in the war, they have to look for jobs outside the home for the first time.

Other women stay at home looking after small children during the day. It is not easy for them to go and hide when there is trouble. And because they are at home they are the first ones to see trouble coming. "You see how old I am?" asked one woman. "But you cannot run as fast as I do. We cannot just sit in our houses and not go and help. It may well be your child dying there. We take anything we can fight with and we go for it. We have to defend our lives and our homes."

Women also have to deal with the fear of rape during attacks. This is what happened to the Dladla family. A group of about sixteen men with balaclavas hammered on the door at one o'clock at night. When Mrs Dladla opened the door one of these men pointed a gun at her and demanded money. They demanded to see Mrs Dladla's son, who is a member of the UDF-affiliated Youth Congress. Mrs Dladla told them he hadn't been staying at home for many weeks. The men then took it in turns to rape Mrs Dladla and her three daughters. After being raped the women were then forced to stand in the passage and watch as the men set fire to the room where their 102-year-old grandmother was sleeping. She died in the fire.

In spite of these problems, women from Ashdown are very strong. They spoke about the importance of coming together. They said, "Before this fighting started we hardly knew each other in this township. But we have learnt that the only way to be strong is to come together and discuss how best to help each other. Together we support those families who have lost their loved ones. There is one family that we discovered where the mother and the father were killed and the young children were left alone. We each contribute whatever we have to make sure that they survive. We bring anything – mielie meal, sugar, anything really."

The women feel that justice is not done to the killers. The courts just warn them and tell them to stop killing. These vigilantes even come to court with their guns, but they are not arrested. "We have only ourselves to trust," say the women. "We went there to the Attorney General together with other women from different areas in Natal. We went to demand that justice be done. We wanted to know why killers are not arrested."

SPEAK 29, 1990

THE NATAL WAR – The bitter fruit of the apartheid tree

More than 100 000 women, old and young, marched through the streets of Umlazi, Natal, on 3 April this year. The women were angry, frustrated and bitter about the actions of the KwaZulu police in their township. "We demand that they get out of our township," said one woman.

The people in Umlazi have experienced brutal police action in recent times. Thousands all over Natal have been left homeless. More than 3 000 lives have been claimed by this war. The war started in Pietermaritzburg in 1987 when Inkatha impis demanded to see people's membership cards. If you were not a member of Inkatha you were an enemy.

Mama Ngobese from Ntuzuma told us: "It was very quiet in this place until impis from Lindelani, outside Durban, started killing young boys from the neighbouring schools here. They accused the boys of being members of UDF. My son was shot and killed. I reported to the police but nothing was done. These people are ruthless killers. They started the war. The community had to defend itself."

SPEAK 37, 1991
Women of steel

Residents in the Vaal Triangle townships say that over 100 people have been killed in the violence. Boipatong has been particularly badly hit.

Boipatong residents say the violence started after the giant Iscor factory moved its workers from a hostel in Sebokeng into the unused kwaMadala hostel across the road from Boipatong. The workers moved there because they feared attacks. Since then though, the residents of Boipatong say Inkatha has used the hostel to launch attacks against the township. Iscor has denied this, but residents of Boipatong are adamant that they have seen strangers going in and out of the complex.

Then on 3 July 1990, the home of a local ANC activist was attacked and his wife, daughter and grandchild murdered. This was the final straw for the women of Boipatong. "We knew then that we had to do something," said local activist Beauty Silela. "So many people have been killed, and the killers are using the hostel right next door to us. We knew we would never have peace as long as they lived next door to us."

Together with the Women's Ministries of the Vaal Council of Churches they decided to organise a march to demand an end to the killings. They handed a memorandum to the Iscor management. In the memorandum the women said the hostel was used as a springboard for terrorist attacks against residents. They called on Iscor to stop harbouring "these enemies of the peace".

Iscor management invited the women to a meeting. They told the women that only Iscor workers were staying at the hostel, but the women said they didn't believe that. "These people have been our neighbours before," Beauty told SPEAK, "and we weren't enemies. So why would we be enemies now? People have reported seeing white men in kombis going in and out of the complex."

Management agreed to organise a meeting between them and the hostel-dwellers to talk about their fears. This meeting had not happened at the time of writing this article. Beauty said that the meeting was important. "We have to do something to stop this violence," she said. "Maybe if we women raise our voices loudly enough then the violence might end."

Women take a stand against violence *by Thandeka Mbuli*

Violet Mncube lives in Thokoza. She is one of many women who have come face to face with the horror of the violence on the East Rand. When Mncube was invited to attend a march organised by women, she did not hesitate. On 27 October 1993, she and a thousand other women from Thokoza marched on the offices of the ANC because they had had enough. Enough of the violence in their communities. They say the ANC has not done enough to help their communities deal with the violence.

The women demanded an end to the meaningless killings that have claimed the lives of more than 1 300 people in less than a year. They also wanted the Internal Stability Unit (ISU) out of the township. The ISU was sent to keep law and order but is instead partly to blame for the breakdown of law and order.

Mncube will do anything to ensure other women do not experience what she did last September. She was lucky to escape with her life. Another woman was not so lucky. "I was on my way home with my grandson after visiting my husband's mother. I got into a taxi at Natalspruit hospital." On the way a man indicated to a driver to turn off the road. "The driver did as told and drove into the KwaMadala hostel. We got scared and started shouting at the driver to let us out. He just drove on. I saw a green police van parked at the side of the gate. Four white ISU policemen with guns were standing outside the vehicle."

The taxi parked behind an ISU car. Two white policemen with guns got out of the car. One stood in front and the other behind the taxi. Mncube and other woman passengers were ordered into a room. A woman with a machine gun sat on the floor and five men stood against a wall. "We were told to take off our clothes, and while we were taking off our clothes members of the police came in to pick out their victims." At this time Mncube's grandson started crying. To her surprise she was told to go.

"As I grabbed my clothes, a woman who knew me grabbed my hand and told me to say goodbye to her family for her. She was not crying, she was just sad. When I walked through the gates a policeman pointed a gun at me and said, 'You must have prayed hard. No ANC supporter gets out of here alive.'"

Mncube was so afraid she only told her family of the incident the next day. She went to the woman's home to give her family the message. "When I got to her house I was told the family had found the woman's body in the Germiston mortuary." Police claim the body was found in the veld.

"People say we want chaos and lawlessness when we demand we want the ISU out of the townships."

Three women who spoke at the march accused the ISU of breaking into their houses, damaging their property, raping women, pointing guns at children, arresting people and not informing their families of their arrests. The marchers called on the ANC to help them remove the ISU from their communities.

ANC Women's League members call for an end to violence – April 1991.

Photo: Elmond Jiyane, CDC Photo Unit

It is not easy to find out how many women have been raped, because, as a field-worker in the area told SPEAK, women are scared and ashamed to tell people about it.

This march was followed by a demonstration outside the multi-party negotiations in November, when community members from the East Rand presented a statement to the negotiating council. "The government of the National Party had let loose their security forces to harass, torture, rape, arrest and kill our people in Thokoza and Kathlehong. The life of a black person has become very cheap in the eyes of the government. We have had enough of their barbaric methods and we are making a plea that they should leave us in peace and not in pieces."

Struggles Today

Many of the struggles women speak of in the previous articles are struggles they continue to wage today. What has changed is the political context. In the place of a hostile government there is now a government which represents the majority of South Africans. However, everyday life for most South Africans has not changed very much.

The battle today is to search out ways to influence the ANC government's agenda in order to ensure that basic needs, essential services and women's rights to resources and decision-making are met. A key strategy in this battle has been to ensure that women are in positions of influence within this new government.

Two interviews conducted in 1996 reflect some of the concerns experienced by women who work in communities. The first interview was with a group of women from the Women's Institute for Leadership, Democracy and Development (WILDD). They talk of the importance of leadership training for women in order to make sure they can take an active part in politics, because this is where power is.

The second interview is with Mmatshilo Motsai, who served as the gender co-ordinator in the government's Reconstruction and Development Programme, and who deals with violence against women in her work in ADAPT in Alexandra township outside Johannesburg. She talks of the need for black working-class women to reclaim their strong, loud voices that were heard during the struggle against apartheid, but which seem to be silent today. We must continue working for the liberation of working-class people and women, she says, or else we will, as a country, simply go the route of the rich becoming richer.

Both interviews highlight the necessary links between women in parliament and women in communities.

The Women's Institute for Leadership, Democracy and Development (WILDD) was set up by women who had been active in the Federation of Transvaal Women (FEDTRAW) during the days of apartheid. WILDD is made up of 32 groups. It has three arms – Women Against Women Abuse, the Young Women's Project and the Development and Democracy Project.

WILDD was the brainchild of Mallie Fakir from Eldorado Park, who had spearheaded FEDTRAW's pre-schools project in the past. "We talked with other FEDTRAW women," said Mallie. "We knew from our years of working together that women had that spirit of working together and doing things. Politically we were about to be free. But so many issues needed to be addressed. Women were very lost. FEDTRAW was not there any more. Something else needed to be done."

FEDTRAW and other UDF-aligned women's organisations were disbanded after the unbannings of the ANC and other liberation parties. These women's organisations had undertaken community projects, and their demise, in Mallie's view, created a vacuum. WILDD was set up to meet needs that were not being addressed.

Mallie pointed out the difference between WILDD and FEDTRAW. She said WILDD is "not a women's movement as such. FEDTRAW had addressed things from a political platform. This had left out a lot of other (non-political) women with similar problems who could contribute. Our vision for WILDD was not a political platform, although the women who founded it came from a political background and political organisations."

While FEDTRAW played a role in mobilising women in the struggle against apartheid at the same time as it organised community projects, WILDD plays a role in training women to take up leadership positions. "We teach women how to run meetings, to participate, to argue constructively. To be politically clear. We've got to train women so there may be many women leaders from grassroots." Women leaders are needed in parliament, in government structures and in the community, and it is WILDD's desire to see black women from working-class communities in these positions.

"My wish is that WILDD could survive and educate grassroots women. My wish is these women should be educated and fight for themselves. They must know their rights and say what they want.

"Power lies in politics. We must not fool ourselves. Unless women get involved in the political process we will get left behind. I would urge women to go back and build wherever they came from and educate."

The women in WILDD regret that there was not sufficient emphasis on training women in the past. They have a sense of their own missed opportunities as activists who were in and out of jail and who missed the chance of formal education. "In the past we did not have time to educate. We fought and we got left behind." WILDD wants to redress this lack so that positions of power are held by more women with grassroots experience.

Mmatshilo Motsei, who shares WILDD's view on the importance of training women, says one of the main tasks confronting women in South Africa today is to increase the "pool of skilled well-informed women on the ground.

"Power comes from the ground," says Mmatshilo. "It is potential power. There is a need to remind people that they have power. As a black woman I believe I have a responsibility to working-class black women. A few black women in positions of power will not make a difference. We need a pool of black women on the ground – African, Indian and coloured – but more-so African women in townships and rural areas."

Mmatshilo says the main issues confronting women today are issues such as violence, economic empowerment and literacy. What is needed, she says, is "grassroots-based community empowerment to make sure women are active participants in the development process – in the social, economic and political arenas. Such work will be an investment for the future so that you have people on the ground who are skilled, confident to raise their voices and informed of what is happening.

"We need to balance the different levels where women are at. We need women in the (parliamentary) Finance Committee who understand gender so that they can influence the budget process. We need women in parliament to influence the debates there. But the focus must be grassroots-based.

"We need to build confidence amongst ourselves as South African women. We must learn from our mistakes. We must reclaim our strong voice. We were so visible as women in the past. Dating back from the women's march to the Union Buildings. We have records of very strong statements made by women throughout time. We have to reclaim that. We must reclaim our strength in development with the same vigour as we did in the struggle against the apartheid regime.

"The hard work has to start – fighting for liberation was clear. Reconstructing is difficult. In a sense we can recognise that reconstruction is a huge challenge that can unite us. We need to work harder during this transition period.

"We must continue working for the liberation of women and working-class people. There is a danger that we are going the route of the rich becoming richer. We must avoid this.

"We need to continue working at different levels. The issues today are different from the issues in the past." Mmatshilo believes women need to look to the achievements of women in parliament. "We need to keep track of the victories we have won. It is a victory that women are occupying positions they never occupied in the past. It is important to talk about the women at the top, to talk of their constraints – they do not necessarily have the power to make changes."

But, says Mmatshilo, "We should go beyond talking about victories. We need to talk about the kinds of networks and strategies we need for women to work together effectively."

SAY NO – Gcina Mhlope

Say No, Black Woman
Say No
When they call your jobless son a tsotsi
Say No

Say No, Black Woman
Say No
When they call your husband at the age of 60
a boy
Say No

Say no, Black Woman
Say No
When they rape your daughter
in detention and call her a whore
Say No

Say No, Black Woman
Say No
When they call your white sister
a madam
Say No

Say No, Black Woman
Say No
When they call your white brother
a baas
Say No

Say No, Black Woman
Say No
When they call a trade unionist
a terrorist
Say No

Say No, Black Woman
Say No
When they give you a back seat
in the liberation wagon
Yes Black Woman
a Big No

THE DANCER – Gcina Mhlope

Mama
they tell me you were a dancer
they tell me you had long
beautiful legs to carry your graceful body
they tell me you were a dancer

Mama
they tell me you sang beautiful solos
they tell me you closed your eyes
always when the feeling of the song
was right, and lifted your face up to the sky
they tell me you were an enchanting dancer

Mama
they tell me you were always so gentle
they talk of a willow tree
swaying lovingly over clear running water
in early spring when they talk of you
they tell me you were a slow dancer

Mama
they tell me you were a wedding dancer
they tell me you smiled and closed your eyes
your arms curving outwards just a little
and your feet shuffling in the sand;
tshi tshi tshitshitshitha, tshitshi tshi tshitshitshitha
O hee! how I wish I was there to see you
they tell me you were a pleasure to watch

Mama
they tell me I am a dancer too
but I don't know ...
I don't know for sure what a wedding dancer is
there are no more weddings
but many, many funerals
where we sing and dance
running fast with the coffin
of a would-be bride or a would-be groom
strange smiles have replaced our tears
our eyes are full of vengeance, Mama

Dear, dear Mama,
they tell me I am a funeral dancer

Graphic: Sanna

CHAPTER TWO

Women Workers

By 1983, women workers were making their voices heard within trade unions. The trade unions which had started after the 1973 strikes were becoming stronger, and by 1983 women in trade unions were speaking out about the issues which concerned them.

The new trade unions of the 1970s were militant, fighting unions bringing black factory workers together all over South Africa. Such unity on the factory floor had not been seen since the 1960s when the South African Congress of Trade Unions (SACTU) had organised workers. SACTU was linked to the South African Communist Party (SACP) and the African National Congress (ANC), and had organised workers in the 1950s and 1960s. Although there were very few women in factories in the days of SACTU, some women workers, such as nurses, were involved in some SACTU campaigns. In the 1960s, SACTU had been banned together with the ANC and the SACP. SACTU leaders had been banned, imprisoned and murdered, and some had gone into exile. SACTU unions had effectively been stopped from organising within the country.

A number of trade unions, called "sweetheart unions" because they were in bed with the bosses, continued to organise white, Indian and coloured workers during the 1960s and 1970s. But most African workers were not allowed to form trade unions. African workers faced great hardships. The government's job reservation policies made sure African workers were restricted to the most menial of jobs. Their wages were low and their working conditions extremely difficult.

In 1973, African workers came out on strike in large numbers. They had had enough of hardship and wanted to see real changes in the workplace and in the country as a whole. The first of the new fighting unions were set up soon after these strikes, and these trade unions were to join together in a new federation, the Federation of South African Trade Unions (FOSATU), which was later to bring in a larger number of trade unions to form the Congress of South African Trade Unions (COSATU).

It was male workers who were involved in the 1973 strikes and, although by then there were greater numbers of women working in factories, the first of the fighting unions were made up of male workers. This was because they were set up in industries in which there were very few women – such as the brick-making industry and the docks. But as the number of fighting unions grew, more and more women became union members, and they began to speak out on their specific issues.

Women workers spoke out on issues such as maternity leave, sexual harassment, the double shift of housework and a job, and husbands and boyfriends who made it difficult for women to attend meetings.

Through their involvement in trade unions, women were winning demands for higher wages, better working conditions and maternity leave. And joining the unions highlighted other struggles – the struggle at home and the struggle within trade unions themselves.

Women began to see that if hard labour at work could be changed, why not change things in the home as well? Women spoke of "taking the struggle home".

Some husbands did not allow their wives to take part in trade unions. They were unhappy about them going to meetings or participating in strikes – and they had the power to stop them. Sometimes this power took the form of intimidation and physical violence.

Within trade unions there were very few women organisers, and the few there were were expected to bring the tea for the male organisers. Women spoke out about their struggles to get women into leadership. They also complained about sexual harassment within the unions from union members and officials. They spoke out about their struggles to get women into leadership.

Women in trade unions organised themselves so that they could take up these problems. At a FOSATU education workshop in 1983, Grace Monumadi called for a women's group within FOSATU as a place where women workers and organisers could gain more confidence. As she said, "We don't want to wake up in years to come to find that women are left out of the struggle."Women's groups were soon set up within FOSATU, later within COSATU, and also within individual trade unions.

It was women factory workers who were most active in these forums. While there was a trade union for domestic workers, this was weaker than the unions of factory workers. Domestic workers were not very active within COSATU. Their working conditions were very different from factory workers: domestic workers in full-time employment worked a nine to twelve-hour day and often lived in, and their movements were therefore far more controlled by their employers.

Women made many gains within COSATU over the years. Among these gains was a major campaign in 1990 to highlight child care needs to employers. The campaign successfully involved men and women workers and got men thinking of child care as their responsibility too. During these years paternity leave was being negotiated increasingly with companies.

With the unions addressing issues such as child care and paternity leave, matters that were seen to be women's issues became issues for all workers. Separate women's forums continued to be important spaces in which women could get some issues on the table. Women met not only in local forums but also in national conferences. COSATU's second National Women's Congress in 1992 noted that because of their domestic burden women could not fully participate in the economy and society. The congress called for a family code on domestic work, wage policies that were fair to women, and women's representation at all levels of the economy and society.

Yet it was difficult to get trade unions to take on many of women's concerns, and at times resolutions on women's rights led to much heated debate without getting anywhere. One such example is the sexual harassment resolution brought to a COSATU congress in 1989 and reported in this chapter from SPEAK 25. This proved yet again that men were in control and that women had to fight hard within COSATU to get their issues taken seriously.

By 1990, men in COSATU were wanting to "do away with women's forums" as they did not see "why women should meet separately".

In a 1992 article in SPEAK, included in this chapter, Maggie Magubane, a woman who had been active in trade unions for years, asks in frustration, "How much longer are women going to be seen as minors – even by our political organisations and trade unions?" All the resolutions passed at every trade union congress are "only paperwork", she says. "These resolutions are never put into practice. Afterwards we have to listen to male comrades saying there is no way they can be led by a woman." Maggie points out that men do not take women's views seriously, and that they use the argument of tradition to keep women down. She believes this "tradition business" must change if we are really striving for liberation. "Customs are only beliefs. We need to create new traditions and customs if we are serious about building a truly new South Africa."

The struggle for women in trade-union leadership continues today. The leaders of present trade unions are still mainly male. While women have gained seats in parliament, putting South Africa among the countries with the highest women's representation, women are far behind in trade-union leadership.

History was made when Connie September became vice-president of COSATU in September 1993, making her the first ever woman national office-bearer in COSATU. Yet by 1994, while women made up 36% of COSATU's membership, only eight per cent of national and regional executive committee members were women. The COSATU 1994 congress debated a quota system as a way of ensuring greater numbers of women in leadership. But this was not passed. Instead, other measures were agreed upon to ensure more women in leadership: special training programmes to build women's participation and leadership, the inclusion of gender in all education programmes, a study on the position of women in trade unions, and monitoring of the situation. Some of these measures are only beginning to be put in place.

COSATU organised mainly in the larger factories. The vast majority of domestic workers, farm workers and informal-sector workers were therefore untouched by the rise of the trade-union movement. And it is in these sectors that the vast majority of women workers are to be found.

A union for domestic workers was launched in 1987. But this has always been a weak union struggling to organise women workers who are paid very low wages, who are cut off from each other in individual homes, and whose long working days and live-in conditions make attending union meetings very difficult. At its launch, the South African Domestic Workers' Union (SADWU) promised to give a voice to workers whose working conditions often resemble slavery. SADWU was affiliated to COSATU but was too weak to make an impact within the larger organisation. By 1996 SADWU had disbanded and today COSATU is looking at possible ways of meeting some of the needs of domestic workers – through setting up advice centres, for example, or by integrating domestic workers within other unions.

Women pavement-sellers are today being organised through the Self-Employed Women's Union (SEWU) in Durban, the Western Cape and the Eastern Cape, and through the Gauteng Self-Employed Women's Union (GASEWU) in Gauteng. An article on SEWU in this chapter highlights some of this union's work.

Women farm workers are being organised in the Western Cape by the Women on Farms Project. In other parts of the country, NGOs set up to work with farm workers are increasingly shifting attention to women on farms as a specific grouping. Women activists from three such NGOs – the Women on Farms Project, the Farm Workers' Research and Resource Centre and the Eastern Cape Agricultural Research Project – organised a national conference in 1995, bringing women from farms from all over South Africa together for the first time to share experiences and look at ways of lobbying for their interests within national policy agendas. One thousand women attended provincial workshops leading to the conference and many went back to their local areas to continue their work through local organisations.

While the laws of the new South Africa, such as the Labour Relations Act and the Basic Conditions of Employment Act, do cover domestic and farm workers, these legal changes have not yet been translated into reality. Many domestic and farm workers do not even know of the changes in the law. Those who are informed are not able to push for change because they are isolated in individual households and on individual farms. Unless these workers are organised, changes in the law will mean little for them. And these women work in sectors which are difficult to organise.

The articles that follow from the pages of SPEAK between 1982 and 1994 capture some of the struggles of the past. Hopefully they may serve as inspiration for the tasks that confront us in the present. The articles are arranged in sub-themes, which include women at work, women on strike, domestic workers, workers as parents and women in FOSATU and COSATU.

Women at Work

In the following articles women workers talk about their problems and the impact of trade unions in their lives.

SPEAK 3, 1983
Carnation women speak about their union

Women workers from Carnation Foods, a factory in Durban organised by the African Food and Canning Workers' Union, shared some of their experiences with SPEAK:

"When we were first approached by the union we were afraid. We were afraid of the police and of losing our jobs. But we started joining up and now most of the workers in the factory are members of the union. Through the union we have won higher wages and better overtime rates for all workers, ten public holidays a year, and five months maternity leave. We have women shop stewards and women on the branch committee of the union. We find that it is difficult for us women workers to attend union meetings. These meetings are at night and we are afraid of our husbands. To help women shop stewards some meetings are held at their homes. But then one husband still got angry with his wife. He said, 'Why do they all come to meet in our house? You must be the ringleader if they all come here.' We must still organise our husbands."

SPEAK 6, 1984
Things are going our way at OK

The Commercial Catering and Allied Worker's Union (CCAWUSA) was one of the first unions in South Africa to negotiate a good maternity agreement. In some stores women workers have won twelve months leave and are assured of a job on the same salary scale when they come back.

Women shop stewards at OK Bazaars said: "The important thing is that now you don't have to choose between a baby and a job. Now it is possible for us to take time off to have a baby, knowing that when we come back to work we'll still have our job – and without any drop in salary or loss of benefits. But if there were no women shop stewards things would slide backwards again. Some store managers don't tell workers about the maximum benefits, or they will say, 'One year is a long time, wouldn't it be better to come back after six months?' So the worker feels she had better come earlier just in case. We must put a stop to this kind of intimidation – and women shop stewards are much more likely to do that. Because we are the ones who understand how a woman feels."

Sweeping the streets of KwaMashu

In October 1984 the women street-sweepers of KwaMashu decided it was time they did something about their low wages and bad working conditions.

"There are about 300 of us sweeping streets. Twenty-eight of us work in the hostels and clean public toilets. Before 1981 men did this work. They were paid R200 a month. Women started at R43 a month – and now it is only women who sweep the streets. The only man now is the induna. When we took these jobs they told us that the job was for one to two hours. We thought we could do washing or other jobs for extra money when the two hours were over. But the job is now from 9 a.m. to 2 p.m., five days a week. We get no sick-leave, no holiday leave. We get no workman's compensation. We don't have adequate protective clothing.

"Our job is to pile rubbish for the trucks to pick up – juba boxes, scrap cars and furniture, bottles and tins. We have to burn some of this. It is almost always windy and this makes it dangerous. We have to duck the flames. One woman was badly burnt when her dress caught alight. Her underclothes stuck to her and she had to be rushed to the hospital. One woman broke her teeth when a studio couch slipped from their hands. Another woman lost her sight in one eye through an accident while working.

"We spoke to the induna about our problems but he did nothing. Some of us decided to go to the union. Others were afraid. After we went to the union it wrote to Port Natal and wages were put up for the first time in November 1984. When the other women saw those who went to the union still had their jobs they were no longer afraid.

"We are still fighting for higher wages, overalls, holidays and sick-leave. About 40 to 50 of us meet every Saturday to discuss and to sing and dance traditional Zulu and Pondo dances. We have acted out a play and we took part in the May Day meeting, where we danced.

"Most of us are elderly. We are widows or our husbands have left us. We are sole supporters of our families, and often we care for our grandchildren as well. We have to work to get food to eat. And so that our children don't get kwashiorkor. Some of us worked in factories before but lost our jobs, mostly through retrenchments. When we went looking for work at factories they said: 'We don't want old ladies and fat women. We want young ones – those who are fat can't run.'

"It is worse for us because we are women. But we are determined to fight our problems. Now all the women are in the union – WE ARE NOT AFRAID!"

Domestic work is slavery

Elizabeth Tshayinca and her daughter Elsie Mbatha have both worked as domestic workers for many years. Elsie has also worked in a factory and is now planning to earn her living as a hawker. Here they talk about their lives as domestic workers.

Elizabeth: "I've been a domestic worker for more than 50 years. I started at eleven years old, looking after a little girl for a pound a month. I'm now 55 years old. For a long time I was a live-in domestic. My mother looked after my children. It's worse when you live in. No rest, day and night. At night you must come and sit in with their children and you get no pay for this."

Elsie: "You earn peanuts. You get paid more when you work part-time, but you come in once or twice a week and you have to do the whole month's job in a short time. You do the fridge, the stove, the windows and you must finish it in one day. Ayi khona! I'm not a machine. The employer says you get an hour lunch but there's no hour. Instead of sitting down to eat lunch you're rushing to finish this job. You don't even chew nicely – you're just rushing to swallow because you're watching the time. You get up early, you get to work early, but you come home late. That's what makes people unhappy about domestic work. It's slavery. And when I get home I cook for my husband. We come home at the same time. He'll sit down with the paper and wants tea. You'll be a 'girl' again. He is the boss reading the paper. And that makes you fed up."

Andries Raditsela, a shop steward from Dunlop and a respected Chemical Workers' Industrial Union leader, tells in this letter of workers' action on the problem of sexual harassment. Raditsela died in detention in 1985 under "mysterious circumstances".

A word of advice to fellow brothers and sisters in the struggle
JOBS FOR SEX

This is something being done in many factories by personnel officers and training officers to our sisters, our girlfriends and wives. Managements know about it, but they don't do anything about it since it does not affect them as much as it does us workers. We keep on complaining about it, but do nothing ourselves, since our sisters are not willing to help us. They are worried about victimisation and scandals. But we can still do it on our own.

How do women get trapped? Usually women get employed at factories outside working hours, even weekends. During lunch-time you can find the personnel office locked. But after lunch you will see a lady coming out of the very office which was locked.

At Dunlop we realised the training officer sold jobs for sex. We planned to catch him in action. He employed one lady on a Friday, and by Tuesday he called this lady to his office. One union member rushed to his door, found it locked and called the manager. The training officer was caught and fired on the spot. The lady was not fired.

Sexual harassment at work became a union issue. *Graphics: SPEAK and Learn and Teach*

We don't want to be tails – Taking the struggle home

Women members of the National Union of Metal Workers (NUMSA) Local Women Workers' Committee in Tembisa say: "We are oppressed at work and we are oppressed at our location and in our houses. We are sick and tired of this. At work we work hard. There is the machine you have to push. At the same time you must come home and cook and do this and do that. Now the organiser comes to the factory, to tell you to organise and to show you where is the way, what you have to do and where are your rights. Now why should I fight at work against hard labour and for maternity leave and not fight at home? If we women do not fight for ourselves there is nobody who is going to fight for us."

The forgotten people *by Bobby Rodwell*

Farm workers are among the most exploited workers in South Africa. Their work, homes and lives depend on the attitude of individual farmers. During droughts and economic hard times many farm workers are losing their jobs and homes.

"There are no good times. We are the unlucky ones," said Henrietta and Freda Mothibedi.

Freda said, "We work in the kitchen at the farm house from 6 a.m. to 6 p.m. six days a week. We walk to the farm house and back. It is a very long way. We do cleaning, washing and ironing. It is very hard work. At the end of the month I get R55."

Henrietta added: "It is impossible to live on that money. Our husbands also earn very little. At month-end we get a bag of mielie meal, no vegetables. We eat meat once a year at Christmas-time. We are always hungry.

"If we are late from the farm house our husbands will cook and look after the children. We cannot get off from work, even if our children are sick. We have heard of the new laws from the newspapers and other farm workers. But it will not mean anything unless there is a way of making sure that farmers change conditions. Even if we as farm workers know what our rights are, we do not have the power to change things. If we ask for an increase we are told to go. People in townships are lucky they can organise together. We cannot do that on farms. We can say goodbye to a worker who tries to organise on the farm. He will be on the way out.

"Our message to people in the towns and townships is that they must not forget about farm workers. Our lives are very hard. Farm workers are the forgotten people."

Making life work for women

Every year many poor rural women from the Transkei and KwaZulu-Natal leave their families behind to work on Durban's pavements. Because there is no other way to survive they face great risks selling their goods, especially at night – the most dangerous time for the hundreds of women who form the backbone of Durban's informal economy. They risk being attacked, robbed or raped.

Mankito Ngcobo (49) knows about these risks. A veteran of the informal-sector business, she has been a beachfront craft vendor since she was eleven. Ngcobo and two other women were allegedly assaulted by a tourist on the beachfront, leaving her with a blue eye. As president of the Self-Employed Women's Union (SEWU) which was launched in July 1994, Ngcobo now knows she has the right to protection under the law. Her first step was to file charges against the tourist who assaulted her. She also persuaded the other two women to do the same.

Most of SEWU's members live in single-sex hostels or sleep on the street, where they take turns to guard their goods throughout the night. They also have to deal with self-styled "pavement lords" who demand rent for public space. Rain often destroys the women's goods because there is no shelter. And mothers struggle to protect their children from street life.

For years these women have been exploited, harassed by police and have suffered abuse at the hands of criminals.

Through SEWU, the women plan to claim their rights. As Pat Horn, founder member and secretary of SEWU, points out: "Individuals cannot resist, but as a group, they can be empowered. The women think they have no rights. When you talk to some of them about rights, they laugh."

Three months after its launch, SEWU had almost 300 members, most of them self-employed beachfront vendors, muti (medicinal herbs) sellers and home-based workers. This is the first union to bring together self-employed women.

SEWU has already successfully negotiated for a market site near the snake park and the Golden Mile beachfront. The women recently elected a "trade committee" which attends to members' problems and reports back at meetings. The union aims to improve the conditions under which the women work.

Zodwa Khumalo, SEWU's vice-president, speaks with enthusiasm about the new market the city council is considering building for informal traders. "We will have toilets, and shelter for our goods, maybe even a créche for our children. But the market must be at a good spot where our customers will come – near the taxi ranks and train stations. Otherwise we will get no business," says Khumalo.

Horn says SEWU's challenge is "to get the women into non-traditional areas like carpentry and electrification. Most are eager to learn non-traditional skills in order to obtain employment in the Reconstruction and Development Programme's building and electrification programmes."

Women on Strike

Women textile workers on strike in the early 1980s.

Photo: Women's Centre

The following two articles tell of two strikes by women workers which formed part of the struggles to demand union rights and better working conditions.

SPEAK 8, 1985

The friendly SPAR unfriendly to workers

"There are two of us in the bakery section, both of us women. We have to do all the work – loading heavy trays into the oven, taking ready bread rolls out, packing, pricing, selling and cleaning. We cannot take breaks. Our backs are always aching," say the bakery staff.

"Trucks from the warehouse no longer come with workers to offload. We have to do this for no extra pay. Sometimes we have to work till 6 p.m. with no overtime pay," says a packer.

Because of these and other problems, SPAR workers were determined to get their trade union, CCAWUSA recognised by their bosses.

For over a year the bosses delayed progress. They tried to scare the workers by taking down the names of union members and questioning each one. They tried to divide Indian workers from African workers. Indian workers have better jobs than

African workers, they are supervisors and cashiers, and they have a separate cloak-room. The bosses built a new cloakroom for Indian workers, while African workers remained in the dirty, crammed cloakroom.

After many months, talks with the bosses broke down and the workers had had enough. They decided to go on strike. They demanded that the bosses recognise their union without delay, that they get a wage increase of R80 a month, and that two dismissed workers be reinstated. "Somehow the bosses got to know about the strike. They threatened us with lay-offs. They asked us what we were going to do about our children, food and rent. They did not scare us."

On the day of the strike at one SPAR shop the boss opened the door for the cashiers and other Indian workers to come in. A shop steward at this store told us: "Four of the cashiers joined the striking workers outside the shop. The boss came out and accused me of forcing the cashiers to join the strike. I told him he was the one putting fear into the workers. We shouted at each other and he managed to pull two of the cashiers away."

SPEAK 15, 1987
Making our voices heard

In 1987, 11 000 workers at OK Bazaars and Hyperama went on strike for ten weeks all around the country. They were members of CCAWUSA. The strike was, at the time, the longest strike of shop workers ever in South Africa.

For many of the workers it was their first time to strike. We asked them if it was harder for a woman to be on strike than for a man. Abigail, a 50-year-old shop steward, is a widow. She said, "If my husband was still alive I don't think it would be possible for me to be as involved in the union as I am. My husband didn't want me to move at all. Not even to work. Only to go to church and the market."

Wendy is 35 years old. She lives in Wentworth with her three children and her husband. She told us, "It's hard for women to be on strike. The man feels he wants to be head of the home with the women under." Wendy's husband did not want her to be a shop steward. When the workers elected her, he was up in arms. He said, "Now that means that you won't be here to see to us." Her husband will not allow her to go to meetings in other towns. She said, "Yes, I do feel frustrated. I would not have married him if I had known he was going to be like this. If I say to him 'We've run out of milk,' he'll say 'go and ask your union', or 'I never asked you to go on strike.' Most of the time I just keep quiet, otherwise it will end up in blows."

Ruby got arrested on the very first day of the strike. How did she feel? "I was so brave! I never thought I'd be as brave as I was during the strike. The policeman said, 'I'll arrest you.' And I replied, 'Its up to you.'"

Abigail said, "Being on strike changed my life. Whenever I step into the doors at OK my heart just tells me there's still a lot of struggling to do. I must be brave because those bosses have got so many tricks."

There are many problems but the women mean to change things. As Colleen said, "These things will be overcome. Most definitely they will. How? By us going out and making our voices heard."

Domestic Workers

Since large numbers of women in South Africa work as domestic workers, and because they are among the most exploited, SPEAK has focused on domestic workers over the years.

SPEAK 13, 1987
SADWU launched

A new union has been born! Domestic workers' organisations have joined together to form the South African Domestic Workers' Union (SADWU). The union represents 50 000 domestic workers around the country. SADWU was launched with high spirits and determined resolutions. It is demanding laws to protect domestic workers, living wages of R200 a month, pensions, workmen's compensation, unemployment insurance, sick-leave and pay, maternity benefits and holiday pay. SADWU has decided to join COSATU.

SPEAK 18, 1988
THULA BABA – A book on domestic workers

A book published by Ravan Press in 1988 tells about the lives of domestic workers.

Ntombi, a 33-year-old domestic worker, writes about herself and her friends. The hardest problem they face is that they cannot be mothers to their own children.

Ntombi has three children in the homeland. But her last-born, who is only one day old, will stay with her. Ntombi is very happy that she can be a mother to this baby. But she worries that the "madam" may change her mind. She might be forced to send her baby away. Or the police may come and find her baby.

Ntombi's friend Tembi is forced to take a job with a "madam" who lets her keep her child, but pays her less money. Another friend Sibongile is sick with worry, as her son has been boycotting school with other students in the location. He has been arrested by the police. Her "madam" allows her to go to the location to see him.

Ntombi's friend Matshepo is forced to send her baby away. The inspectors have given her 24 hours to take the child to the homelands. The friends feel for each other. They do their best to help each other. They go to the station with Matshepo.

Domestic workers took to the streets to fight for their rights – June 1989.   *Photo: SPEAK*

Ntombi writes: "At five o'clock this morning we walked to the station. It was dark and cold. It was a long walk. We wore blankets to keep warm. We carried our babies on our backs and boxes on our heads. I have walked to the station five times to send a child away. It doesn't matter if it is my own child or a sister's child. I feel the same sickness and sadness in my heart. It is such a terrible thing for a mother to send her child away. It is such a terrible thing for a child to lose her mother.

"For me the saddest thing in my life was to take my children on the train and come back without them. For Matshepo it was even worse. She had taken her first-born home. A month later the baby was dead. I was sick in my heart when I looked at Tshidiso ... he didn't know what was happening. Matshepo did know ... but she had cried her tears last night. She was strong now in the morning."

SPEAK 25, 1989
Domestic workers say no to slavery!

"Employers must realise that the slave trade was abolished a long time ago. They should not treat domestic workers as slaves," said Margaret Nhlapo of the South African Domestic Workers' Union (SADWU).

On 1 June 1989, domestic workers from all over South Africa called for laws to protect domestic and farm workers. They presented petitions to the offices of the Commissioner of Manpower in every city in the country.

SADWU wants contracts between employer and worker, a living wage, pensions, unemployment insurance and an end to child labour. Margaret Nhlapo said: "Domestic workers are still getting paid as low as R50 and R80 a month, which is disgusting. We are demanding R450 a month for skilled workers who can look after small children, cook or bake, or who have worked for a long time and know their jobs well. We are demanding R350 a month for a semi-skilled worker. And these demands are for a five-day, 40-hour week. For casual work we demand R3,50 an hour. Overtime work should be paid for and one month's notice must be given in the case of termination of employment."

SADWU believes that if employers cannot pay these wages they should not employ domestic workers. The employer should provide decent accommodation with hot and cold running water and electricity.

SADWU demands that children under sixteen years of age should not be employed. They have come across many cases of child labour. "It is ridiculous. This happens especially among coloured, Indian and African employers who bring children from the rural areas to work in their homes in town." Recently a child of fifteen was sent to SADWU by a social worker from a township. "She had bruises on her back. We called in her employers – a teacher and a salesman – and told them to send the child to her home.

"Our demands are not only to white employers, but to African, Indian and coloured employers as well. The lifestyle of domestic workers is breaking families.

SPEAK

1989 70c Nº 25

ORGANISE OR STARVE

NO TO SLAVERY
SAY DOMESTIC WORKERS

They have no human rights like giving love to their child. Their children are neglected. A mother can't bring up her child as she would like to. She will see her child once a year. The mother becomes a stranger. That should not be happening. We are humans after all."

SPEAK 38, 1992
The workers hidden in homes by Libby Lloyd

It isn't easy to organise domestic workers. There is no factory floor to visit, only thousands of individual households. The union has to rely on workers hearing about it from friends and neighbours. According to the government there are more than 860 000 domestic workers in South Africa, and only about 23 000 are union members.

Violet Mothlasedi, SADWU president, says that the biggest problem these days is workers being fired. "Employers sometimes say they can't afford to pay. Sometimes they give no reason at all." Some live-in workers can't have visitors in their rooms and their families are not allowed to stay over. Others are locked in by security systems. Their bosses don't trust them with keys so they are prisoners behind high walls.

Violet says white bosses are not the only problem. "Black and Indian bosses sometimes are the worst. In townships workers don't have rooms. They have to sleep in the kitchen or in the children's rooms. They don't even get one hour off. They are on call 24 hours a day, every day of the week."

At present, domestic workers are not included in labour laws. After marches and petitions by domestic workers, the government appointed a committee to look into legal protection for them. The committee's report says domestic workers should be included in the Labour Relations Act and in the Basic Conditions of Employment Act. If this becomes law, domestic workers can take bosses to court for unfair treatment. But it will take a long time for these recommendations to become law. The commission is waiting for comments and some details are still being worked out. The recommendations will then go to parliament to be voted into law. And the recommendations have not included one of the union's major demands – for a minimum wage. This means workers will still be paid peanuts.

Workers are Parents Too!

Workers in the 1990s took up their rights as parents. Some workplaces gave fathers paid time off on the birth of a baby. Workers wanted to bring to bosses' attention that they were parents too, and men workers were challenged to take on the responsibility of caring for children. The next two articles tell of a COSATU campaign on child care and of how one man was able to use his paternity leave to play his role as a parent.

Workers are parents too

Thursday 20 September 1990 was a very important and unusual day for workers, their children and the bosses. Thousands of children went with their parents on buses and taxis to work. The bosses watched as the workers of tomorrow streamed through the factory gates. This day was part of COSATU's national child care campaign.

Patrick Khumalo, a SACCAWU shop steward, said: "We wanted to show the bosses that workers are parents too, and that our children lack proper care."

There are very few crèches and pre-schools in black townships. Those that do exist are expensive and overcrowded, and have few qualified teachers.

Many workers worry about what happens to children during the day. Some children roam the streets. Anything could happen to them. One woman worker said, "I worry about my children all day. I know the aunty I leave them with doesn't give them the food I leave."

Workers say it is time the bosses take some responsibility for child care. "If we want to build a new South Africa with equal opportunities for all, then we must start at the cradle."

The day of action is the beginning of an ongoing campaign. COSATU demands:
• twenty days paid leave a year to take care of children
• a special child allowance from the state for unemployed workers with children
• the right to a family life.

The bosses responded in different ways to the day of action. Some put on a party with sweets and toys and games to play. Others did not like the idea. At Nissan in Rosslyn, workers and their children were locked outside the factory and had to go home. At one branch of Clicks the police were called.

One boss, Mr Lehmbecker, said, "Workers need crèches and the state should be responsible for child care. But private companies should also do something. We will put aside some funds towards a crèche in some way."

While the campaign challenges the bosses, it also challenges male workers to give up the idea that the job of child care belongs to mothers alone. Many men workers took part in this day of action. We asked Patrick Khumalo if this meant that men are changing their attitudes. He said: "Men have realised that child care is also their responsibility. We have included a demand for paternity leave in our national negotiation. Men were in the forefront of that struggle.

"The struggle to get the bosses to see workers as parents is a long one. And so is the struggle to get men to share responsibility for their children. The COSATU Day of Action is just the beginning."

Workers are parents too! Union members took children to work to highlight child care needs, September 1990.   *Photo: SPEAK*

SPEAK 33, 1991
I told them I was here to help my wife

William Matlala works at COSATU head office in Johannesburg. His family lives in Mphahlele location in Pietersburg. William's wife Alinah has recently had a baby and he took six days paternity leave to help her.

William told us, "It was nice because it gave a lot of help to the family. It gave a boost to my relationship with my wife and children. It is important for us to have this time – especially people in rural areas – because we don't see the family often. You bring love to them and this is important. When a woman has a baby she is weak. She needs someone with whom she has a good relationship, especially one who is in love with her. She can tell you things she can't just tell anybody. Also you can get to care for the new baby.

"As a father you shared in bringing this baby into the world and you should know how the pain is, how the baby is and how she is coping."

This new baby is William's fourth child, but this is the first time he has had paternity leave. William said, "I just saw the others when they were about one year old – just for the weekend, maybe spending a day at home. With this one I saw her when she was two weeks old and I did everything that was needed."

We asked William how he spent his paternity leave. He said, "I changed nappies and I fetched water. I was prepared to bath the baby but my wife did not want me to do this. The grandmother said, 'You are here, now we are going.' But they were near enough to call if we should ever need them. The older children were happy that I was home. They wanted me to wash them, prepare their food and take them to school."

William said that it was a very new idea that men should take leave and look after children. He said, "Paternity leave is something that is written down in the agreements with certain companies, but workers don't take it. I am sure they will enjoy it when they do."

Some women workers worry that men would use this leave in the wrong way. They would use it to have a very good time for themselves. William agreed that this was a problem, but he said that in time men would realise the importance of caring for their children.

He said, "We know we are dominant as men. We know we are the superior in the house. From here it will be a long way to reach equality. When a tree is old it is hard to make it young. Men will have to accept that the old way of operating is wrong. They will see that they can get enjoyment from helping their families. They can bring love home. In many families today the children see the father as an enemy. When the father comes in they must leave and sit outside. A man becomes the person who is always demanding and commanding."

William thinks it is only a matter of time before men start using paternity leave properly. "People will get to know this leave. More and more will ask for it at work. And people in the community will make men feel ashamed if they are not using this leave to care for the wife and child."

William is back at work in Johannesburg, far from home. He misses his new baby, his wife and his older children. But his eyes and his voice tell us how happy and excited he is that he was able to share the new baby with his family.

Women in FOSATU and COSATU

The two largest federations of trade unions during the 1980s and 1990s were FOSATU and COSATU. FOSATU was formed in 1975 and in 1985 was instrumental in forming COSATU, together with other unions. Women made their voices heard within these federations, and both organisations played an important role in advancing women's concerns. But many of the problems discussed since 1983 still remain critical problems for women today. As the following articles show, at times there was more debate than consensus on women's concerns. And women workers are afraid that many paper resolutions remain just that – commitments on paper. There is still a long way to go to turn these commitments into action. At the same time, as women in COSATU say, the debates have resulted in greater awareness of women's issues. The following articles trace thinking and action within FOSATU and COSATU conferences.

SPEAK 4, 1984
Share the work with us

In July 1983 FOSATU organised a discussion on women workers.

Tembi Cecilia Nabe of the Metal and Allied Workers' Union (MAAWU) spoke about women in urban areas. "Both the man and wife have to get up in the morning to go to work. But the woman has to get up first to make tea for her husband, get him water to wash and make the bed. And when the man is still washing, the woman has to wash the baby, and take it to the woman who nurses it. And then she has to come back again to prepare herself for work. Remember the woman has to work as a domestic. She has long hours, hard work, is harassed by the madam the rest of the day and she finishes work at 5.30 p.m. She then travels to Soweto. The earliest she can get home is 7.30 p.m. Her husband gets home at 6.30 p.m. He doesn't even think of fetching the baby. He makes it a point that every time he comes back from work his little darling is next to him – that is, his bottle of whisky or brandy.

"When the woman comes she must make a fire and prepare the evening meal. Then she must wash, prepare the bed for her husband, do the ironing, care for the baby and prepare for the next morning. When it comes to bedtime the husband becomes impatient. He says, 'Woza Lapa.' That's the overtime. When she says, 'No, I'm busy; I'm still doing housework' – now there's another problem. The husband becomes angry. And then the woman becomes angry. The following day the husband is not going to come back. He is looking for another woman."

Mama Lydia Kompe spoke about her experiences as an organiser for the Metal and Allied Workers' Union (MAAWU). She joined MAAWU after losing her job while on strike in 1976. "At this time I was the only woman organiser. I encountered many problems, but I coped, because I realised there was no excuse but to cope. I wished I was not married, because the marriage stood right in my way. My feeling is that of all the problems women encounter, marriage is the biggest problem that prevents their involvement in union activity.

"Women have shown real courage and commitment in trade unions. They have the ability of acting and pulling quite strong to make the union work effectively. But up to this date have we ever heard of a woman chairlady of a union? Why? And why is it that not one union has a woman president? I wouldn't expect the answer that it's because it's a woman.

"All these problems need to be taken into serious consideration. A woman is a human being. She needs the assistance of her husband and her family as a human being. And we appeal for equal rights, for God's sake. We don't want to be inferior."

Grace Monamudi spoke about what unions are doing about the problems faced by women workers.

"We negotiate with bosses at the factories for equal wages for men and women, for equal training and for maternity benefits for women. We hope by talking about democracy and equality in the union we will start to change people's attitudes and encourage more participation among women.

"In a FOSATU course recently there was the suggestion that we need to talk more about the problems of women workers, and there should be a women's group within the trade-union movement. This group would be a place where women workers and organisers could gain more confidence.

"We have to be honest in saying that discussions of this problem are very very new in the South African labour movement. But we definitely should not be scared of these problems. We need to start acting now because we don't want to wake up in years to come to find that women have been left out of the struggle. We need to break down every division that exists between men and women workers as quickly as possible."

After the women gave their talks, the audience was asked to join in the discussion. A man said: "That women are exploited in the factory I'll agree. But to say that to make food and fire for her husband and children is exploitation, I cannot agree. It is tradition among our people. It is unacceptable to most of our people that a man should look after children and do the washing."

A woman responded: "We cannot depend on what our forefathers did. There were no unions then. It is high time we change. We must have equal rights. No one is inferior. We are all equals."

Other men also responded. One said: "We don't have to use tradition. If a man is home early he has all the rights to make the fire and look after the children."

Another man said: "Brothers and sisters, it is high time we surrender. If both go out to work but when we get home it is my time to rest and my wife's time to carry on working, I don't think the struggle will go on."

Viva COSATU women viva – COSATU Women's Congress April 1988

For the first time, women workers came together from all over the country to talk about women in the community, the union and at work.

They decided to organise women's forums at local level. They discussed women's health and safety, contraception, abortion, cancer of cervix, sexual harassment, child care and maternity.

They talked about difficulties women had attending meetings and taking part in union work because of housework and child care. They said men should take part in caring for children and in sharing housework. There should be equal relationships between men and women in COSATU and in the country as a whole.

Taking the women's struggle forward

COSATU's first National Women's Seminar was held in March 1989. Women from COSATU affiliates and from community-based organisations attended. Delegates agreed that more must be done to fight for the rights of women workers. They called for more women in COSATU structures. They want to ensure that COSATU's Living Wage Campaign includes women's right to equal pay, to buy a house and to housing loans. Issues of child care and violence against women should be taken up in campaigns. The women discussed the importance of fighting sexual harassment. They got the support of Jay Naidoo, COSATU general secretary, who said: "Forced sex is rape and must be treated as a very serious crime in the struggle. No comrade, no matter how senior he is, should be forgiven for such a crime. He should be isolated from the struggle."

The giant grows – COSATU's resolutions on women

The July 1989 COSATU congress was attended by 1 800 workers and was at the time the biggest congress ever held.

For most of the congress there was a strong sense of unity, and it was clear that the unions meant business in their fight against oppressive labour laws and apartheid. But there was not always unity on the issue of women's oppression.

The resolution that caused the hottest and longest discussion was a resolution on sexual conduct brought to the congress by the Transport and General Workers' Union (TGWU). The debate lasted four hours, and this was the only resolution put to the congress that was not adopted.

The resolution was put forward because of problems experienced in the union. As Jane Barret, general secretary of the TGWU, told us, "When we were planning the resolutions for congress, the president of our union raised the issue of sexual harassment

Women COSATU members organised a march in 1990 against the Labour Relations Amendment Act – which was hostile to unions. *Photo: SPEAK*

and sexual discipline. He felt very strongly about the problem of new women recruits who get exploited by senior union men. The men, including union organisers, use their position to start relationships with new women recruits. The men are not serious about these relationships and when the relationship ends women leave the union. This was a regular pattern and was also happening in other unions. All of this inspired the resolution on sexual conduct. People were saying: The personal is political."

Some at the congress felt this resolution should never have been brought to the congress. Others said the oppression of women is a reality, like racism, and needs to be tackled head on. But since there was not sufficient support to pass this resolution, it was suggested that the issue be referred to the COSATU Code of Conduct which deals with how activists should behave in all areas of life.

COSATU women feel that the resolution has raised an important issue and has started a debate. Dorothy Mokgalo of the National Union of Metal Workers of South Africa (NUMSA) says: "The discussion sparked by the resolution has taken us a step forward. It has created awareness."

There is clearly a need for more discussion and education on the problems of sexism, sexual harassment and the power men have over women in our society.

Among the resolutions passed at the congress were resolutions to end sexist language in the COSATU constitution, to build a national women's organisation, and to ensure women are in leadership at all levels of the organisation. A woman's sub-committee will be set up to ensure that the resolutions passed will be put into action.

SPEAK 29, 1990
Nobody can stop the river

In April 1990, women from the COSATU Wits region organised a march of over 3 000 people, mostly women, to protest against the new Labour Relations Amendment Act (LRA). Workers all over the country had rejected the act for its hostility to the trade-union movement.

Women had the idea for this march, and it was women who organised it. "We did it because we could see that things were becoming bad without the women. Women also want to be free," said one of the marchers.

Male comrades were enthusiastic about the march. One of them said, "This is making history. We are saluting the women." The march was important because it showed men and women that women can be leaders. As one of the organisers said, "It is important that we motivate women to come up, to take up leadership, to be active in the union and in the organisation as a whole." More actions like this will encourage more women to take their rightful place in the decision-making bodies at every level.

In the words of one of the women, "Nobody can stop the river from flowing; we are going forward."

SPEAK 31, 1990
Women workers must organise

Sibongile Masangwane and Kally Forest of the Transport and General Workers' Union (TGWU) told SPEAK of the importance of women's forums. "This is where we learn to talk, approach issues and to debate," said Sibongile. "Some are still very shy. They cannot talk about rape, love affairs or abortion in front of male comrades." Kally said: "Women talk more when they are on their own about the LRA (Labour Relations Act) or the Worker Charter. They feel more confident. But the problem is that very few women attend the forums." Women are bogged down with housework. Men don't share in this.

Sibogile said: "Many women do not have the support of their husbands or boyfriends. If husbands don't let you go to meetings you must stay at home and not work. Let's see if he is going to manage."

A time to push ahead

SPEAK met some members of the women's sub-committee of COSATU's National Education Committee (NEDCOM). We met comrades Maggie Magubane, Dorothy Mogalo, Elizabeth Thabethe, Tiny Mabena, Rafilwe Ndzuta and Rachmat Omar.

COSATU women believe now is the time to work hard at organising women workers. They believe that women workers should play an important part in building a new, non-racial, non-sexist, democratic South Africa.

They said: "It is important to organise women in COSATU. Especially now with the reviving of the ANC and the ANC Women's League. The ANC is a multi-class organisation. If women workers are not organised their voices will not be heard within these organisations. We cannot rely on the ANC Women's League to raise basic demands in factories and workplaces. Women's forums in COSATU and its affiliates must still remain on the ground.

"The main aim of the women's sub-committee is to make sure that women are active at all levels in the unions and in COSATU, and especially at leadership levels. The second aim is to encourage women to come to meetings to discuss their problems as women.

"There are very few women in leadership positions in most of the unions. This means women's issues are left out of discussion or are put at the very bottom of the agenda. Most of our problems are not being taken up seriously. This will change if women are organised and push for our demands."

In addition to fighting the bosses, women in unions have to fight the attitudes of male comrades. Most men in the unions do not understand the problems of women workers. Sometimes men laugh when a woman gets up to talk about women's problems in a meeting.

"Some male comrades are trying to do away with women's forums. They say the only place women are seen is in the forums. They say women should stop working as a separate group, and that women's issues are not being made part of the unions themselves. They say, for example, if sexual harassment is only discussed in forums and not in the union, how will we reach men on these issues? These male comrades seem to be taking things backwards.

"Not enough time is being given for the women's forums to develop. Within COSATU we are still having problems developing education structures although these have been going for a much longer time than the women's forums. But no one is saying that education structures must close down. With the women's forums after only a year and a half we are being criticised."

Women's forums are making progress. As a result of them there are more women in leadership in COSATU and its unions. More women are attending meetings, women are developing and women's issues are being discussed more widely.

But it is not easy for women to get to meetings. "Women don't have enough time because of responsibilities at home. They have difficulties attending weekend and evening meetings. Male comrades can attend till midnight or the whole weekend and no one will ask them, 'Where do you come from?'"

The women see their real fight as a struggle against cultural practices. "Lack of training and education for women is partly a problem. But the real thing is cultural background. Even though a woman is educated she is told, 'You are a woman.' And women have the idea that they are 'just women' and that men must be in the forefront. Men think they cannot be told what to do by women. Men also need education so that they change the way they see women."

The women know their struggle is a long and difficult one. They push ahead in challenging the attitudes of men comrades in their unions and in organising more and more women workers. They are fighting for more women in leadership, for more women to talk out about their lives, and to make sure that the problems of women workers will not be ignored in the new South Africa.

SPEAK 40, 1992

Paper work *by Maggie Magubane*

Maggie Magubane has been active in the trade-union movement for sixteen years. She writes about her anger with paper commitments to non-sexism.

"How much longer are women going to be seen as minors – even by our political organisations and trade unions? At every trade union congress, resolutions are passed saying the union will fight all forms of discrimination and promote participation and leadership by women. This is only paperwork. These resolutions are never put into practice ... Afterwards we have to listen to male comrades saying there is no way they can be led by a woman. We have to listen to certain shop stewards insisting women can't be elected as office bearers – it is against tradition.

"Despite the resolutions there are still union organisers who believe it is your duty as a woman to make tea for them in the office.

"In meetings, women's views are not taken seriously. Sometimes you find when a woman stands up to talk, the men will make funny remarks or whistle at her before she even opens her mouth. Many women won't talk in meetings because of this. When a woman does raise a point she is often ignored. But if later in the discussion a male comrade makes the same point the meeting will applaud him. Often a male comrade will wait until after a meeting to congratulate you or ask you to explain your point.

"Yet when you look at all the work done by women – in the home and in the workplace – you see how much we contribute. The men are seen as the heroes, but often it is thanks to the women that they get this recognition.

"As a concerned woman I ask myself, 'Is it worthwhile for women to attend meetings when our views are not considered?' Are we in the trade-union movement really striving for liberation? If so, when are we going to change this tradition business?

"Customs are only beliefs. We need to create new traditions and customs if we are serious about building a truly new South Africa."

74

SPEAK 43, 1992
COSATU's second National Women's Congress *by Thoraya Pandy*

COSATU's second National Women's Congress, held in August 1992, raised the following issues: economic independence for women, land ownership, legal status, taxation, equal pay for work of equal value, and women's employment in public works programmes. Delegates noted that because of the domestic burden, women cannot fully participate in the economy and society. They called for a family code on domestic work, wage employment policies that are fair to women, and women's representation at all levels of the economy and society.

SPEAK 58, 1994
From the factory floor *by Thoraya Pandy*

In September 1993 Connie September became COSATU vice-president, and for the first time ever COSATU had a woman national office-bearer. She said: "I think we should be encouraged that we are beginning to enter areas which were controlled by men. COSATU must develop a more intense programme on the grassroots level to empower women."

Women delegates at COSATU's second Women's Conference in August 1992.
Photo: Elmond Jiyane, CDC Photo Unit

75

Building union women *by Deanne Collins*

Another COSATU congress goes by with resolutions on women's participation and leadership in the unions.

Women make up 36% of COSATU membership. Only eight per cent of its national and regional executive committee members are women – not counting SADWU, the union for domestic workers, where women are a majority.

Despite all the resolutions passed over the years at COSATU congresses, there is still a long way to go to turn resolutions into reality.

Most delegates to the COSATU congress in September 1994 were men. Very few women took part in discussion. It was only when gender issues came up that women's voices were heard.

One debate was whether the unions should have a quota system, where a number of leadership positions would be set aside for women. Arguments against the quota system were that people should be elected on merit. In the end congress did not accept the quota system. Instead a resolution was passed to build women's participation and leadership within COSATU.

Congress decided on special training programmes for women shop stewards, staff members and leaders; including gender in all education programmes; getting COSATU's CEC to monitor this programme; a study conducted by the research institute on the position of women in the unions; and strengthening women's structures within the federation.

Struggles Today

Many of the problems women talked about over the years continue in the present. Patricia Appolis, national gender co-ordinator of the South African Commercial Catering and Allied Workers' Union (SACCAWU), an affiliate of COSATU, spoke of some of the issues of concern to women in trade unions in 1997. Most significantly these include women making their mark in leadership, and in the policy debates of the day. Appolis also highlights some of the gains made over the years.

With Appolis' appointment as gender co-ordinator in 1994, SACCAWU was the first COSATU affiliate to appoint a full-time gender co-ordinator. At the time of this interview there were four COSATU unions with full-time gender co-ordinators: NUMSA, PPWAWU, SACCAWU and SARHWU.

Among the gains won within SACCAWU since her appointment, Appolis lists the following: "The culture of the union is changing. It is more gender-sensitive internally. Reports and recommendations on gender are interrogated, but accepted. These issues are taken more seriously, and people are more sympathetic and accepting.

"We are conducting research on child care. The research team is working out concrete guidelines for one company and will take their proposal to the company. We are negotiating with companies on parental rights."

Patricia is a member of the COSATU women's sub-committee. "As COSATU we have done a lot of work. We have adopted practical resolutions, adopted the COSATU Code of Conduct, developed research and employed a researcher. We commission research. And we run a basic women's leadership course which is integrated into the main COSATU education programme. COSATU women have a representative on NEDLAC's labour chamber and on the Commission for Gender Equality."

Patricia reflected on the challenges confronting women workers within COSATU. Among these is the need to make an impact in national policy debates, most crucially around the government's macro economic policy. COSATU's contribution to the national macro economic agenda was put out in a document entitled Social Equity.

"Women were not involved in the Social Equity document. The document was prepared at a fast pace. It is difficult for us to interact with macro economic policy."

The leadership programme hopes to give women the tools so that they can play a more central role in policy. "We will look at women in the economy. At institutions in the labour market."

SACCAWU, the union Patricia works for, is also focusing on building women's leadership. Says Patricia: "In the past gender work in the union concentrated on highlighting specific days – such as a day to highlight child care needs. The focus has now shifted to developing leadership."

Together with Khanya College in Johannesburg, SACCAWU has started educational workshops for women members of the union's local executive committees, the union's national negotiating team and local gender co-ordinators. These women will be part of a three year programme in each of the union's eight regions. Every year for three years these women will attend a week-long workshop. There is a basic gender course, an intermediate course and an advanced course.

SACCAWU intends that the training programme will empower women to play a more central role in the trade union and will result in more women in the leadership of the trade union movement. At present very few women are in leadership even when they make up an overwhelming majority of the workforce.

Patricia says of SACCAWU: "Between 60% and 70% of the union membership are women. There has been an increase in women's employment in this sector."

But there are still struggles to be waged to get women into leadership. "At the SACCAWU congress last year a quota was proposed in order to ensure women are in leadership positions. This was not accepted by the union on the basis of the argument that positions should be filled on merit. The real issue is competition for positions. Men fear they will lose their positions. It is a power thing.

"At present two out of six national office bearers are women. In the regions there are no women regional office bearers. Now two vice-chairs out of eight and two regional treasurers out of eight are women. At the local level there are more women on local executive committees. Women prefer to choose men shop stewards. There are more male shop stewards."

Another COSATU affiliate, the Chemical Workers' Industrial Union, has reserved seats for women. Yet another, NEHAWU, has a ruling that there should be 50/50 male/female representation.

There are many challenges for women workers in the present. These include holding on to the victories of the past, making sure women get into leadership, taking part in policy debates, and spreading organisation to sectors that are not organised.

MADAM – Rosaline Naapo

Madam
remember when I was young
and happy
Remember when I used to
perform
your choruses in time
Remember when I used to run
your errands fast

Today I'm old
I'm no good

Today I'm walking on three legs
I'm no good

Madam
where did my sweat go
Madam did you ever consider
that today I need you
as you needed me
in the sixteen years
I worked for you

CHAPTER THREE

Fighting Violence against Women

Over the years, women have fought violence against women, at times alone and isolated in their homes, at other times together with other women. It was taken up by community women's groups such as the Port Alfred women and the Soweto women who speak out in this chapter, and in the East Rand by women whose voices we have heard in chapter one of this book. It was an issue raised over the years within trade unions through discussion on rape, beatings and sexual harassment. It was an issue that confronted women in the throes of the political violence within communities.

Today violence against women seems to be on the increase. Joanne Fedler of the Tshwaranang Legal Advocacy Centre to End Violence Against Women says:

"Organisations working with survivors of rape and battery comment that the viciousness and cruelty of assaults has become more acute. No longer are women fortunate enough just to be raped and left to become outspoken survivors as in the good old days. Now they are tortured before they are set alight. No longer are our rapists over the age of consent. Boys going through the first throes of puberty rape three-year-old children and then strangle them. Our rapists and batterers have realised that if you snuff out your victim there is no one to testify against you."

(Sunday Times, 10 August 1997)

As Fedler points out, there are many problems in ensuring that rapists are dealt with. The police and the legal system more often than not allow criminals to slip through loopholes. Male judges often make judgements that are against women.

A number of organisations have been set up to fight violence against women. Their work ranges from lobbying the Justice department and training police, to offering counselling and creating public awareness. People Opposed to Woman Abuse (POWA) in Johannesburg has been working in this area for many years. ADAPT, based in Alexandra township near Johannesburg, counsels women and more recently has started a programme to counsel men who are perpetrators of violence. Today there is

79

also an increasing number of organisations dealing with violence against women in rural areas. Various organisations working to fight violence and to give women support have come together in a national network and in regional networks.

The articles from the pages of SPEAK highlight women's struggles against violence over the years.

Women march against violence in Hillbrow, Johannesburg, International Women's Day, 8 March 1991.
Photo: Anna Zimienski

FROM THE PAGES OF *SPEAK*

SPEAK 13, 1986
No to rape, say Port Alfred women *by Kally Forest*

In 1986, the Port Alfred Women's Organisation (PAWO) organised a stayaway to protest against the fact that the police had failed to charge a man who had raped one of their members. SPEAK talked to Koleka Nkwinti from PAWO about the events that followed.

SPEAK: What were PAWO's demands?

KOLEKA: We demanded that the police charge the rapist with rape and assault. If they met our demands we would go back to work. We also demanded that the white women in town come to women in the township. We wanted to show and tell them about our problems in the township. We know that all women, black and white, fear rape. We felt that white women may understand and be sympathetic to us. We also wanted white women with husbands in the police to explain our problems to their husbands.

SPEAK: How did the white community deal with your demands?

KOLEKA: The white women were not sympathetic. We were surprised; we thought they would feel for us. They just got angry, probably because now they had to do their own housework. After a few days the Port Alfred Employers' Federation came to speak to our civic organisation in the township. They did not come to speak to PAWO. So we told our men in the civic – "Please don't negotiate for us. This is a women's problem. Men do not get raped."

The Employers' Federation would not speak to PAWO. But this did not worry us. We wanted to speak to the white women in the town. A week later some English-speaking white women came to PAWO. We decided to meet and talk in the future. That night we called off the stayaway. PAWO members were happy to go on talking to these white women. The rapist was charged with assault, but not rape. But the township people were so angry with him that it was impossible for him to stay in the community.

SPEAK: What happened after the stayaway?

KOLEKA: The next morning the police detained me and three other PAWO members, as well as my husband, brother-in-law and seven other men from the community. The police questioned me about the stayaway. They could not believe that women alone had organised everything. They think that men are behind everything women do. I feel that women of Port Alfred became very strong. I was held in prison far away from Port Alfred. But women hired a car to visit me and bring me food.

SPEAK: Do township men and women talk about rape?

KOLEKA: It is very important to talk openly about the problem of rape. Most people are ashamed and shy. Often the family of the raped girl or woman doesn't want to talk about it. But in Port Alfred it is different. We started organising in our community around education, child care, pensions, and so on. We also talk about any sexual assault on women. Port Alfred people see sexual assault as another kind of oppression. Men and women think the same about this – we are united in the struggle.

A raped woman is trusted. If she says she was raped we support her. It does not matter who she is – even if she is a drunkard and she gets raped, the rape is still a crime against her. In fact it is worse, because she is in a weak position. We do not blame a woman for rape. We do not say that the rape was the woman's fault. So women can talk about sexual harassment openly and they will get community support.

SPEAK 17, 1987
Rape in marriage

There are people who deny that there can be such a thing as rape within a marriage, but during the late 1980s there have been two court cases which have given hope to women who wish to defend themselves against this crime. SPEAK explores this issue.

In September this year a Bloemfontein magistrate found a man guilty of trying to rape his wife. He made his decision because of a new set of bills about sexual crimes. If these bills become law, they will mean some changes for women.

Men should not be allowed to get away with the crime of raping women. Rape should be treated as a crime whether it happens in a marriage or not. Isn't murder a crime within a marriage?

SPEAK asked three students from Khanya College in Johannesburg to go out and talk to people about this issue. The students asked people they met: "Is there such a thing as rape in marriage?"

Maureen is a 22-year-old student. She said, "Yes, there is such a thing. Women have so long been treated as inferiors and as sexpots. I believe that a woman's feelings should be respected. Women sometimes have moods whereby they don't feel like making love. This doesn't mean she doesn't love her husband."

Nathaniel is a 26-year-old student. He said, "Immediately a man marries a woman he has a right over her. Lobola still exists in our society and a woman appears to be a commodity; then when a man has bought that commodity he has a right to have sex with her, even forcefully. He should not be punished for this."

Thembikile believes that men use their wives as an outlet for their frustrations. He said, "You see, men suppress their feelings of anger and frustration … and in order for them to release those feelings they abuse their wives."

We need a new kind of relationship where women and men can communicate as equals. Where men do not see women as their property to use as they wish. And where women demand the right to be treated as human beings.

As Maureen said, "Men should respect their wives as equals, and they have to understand them as partners. If husbands are using violence and force when it comes to the bedroom department, then one gets the idea that he does not love his wife. Action must be taken against such people."

SPEAK 19, 1988
Our men must stop beating us

Mary is sitting in the room with us. We have come to talk to her about wife-beating. Mary has three teenage children. She lives with them and with her husband. Mary wears glasses, but her glasses are badly broken. When she came in she was limping. Her leg looked a very strange shape. It had scars from being beaten. Her husband did this to her. We asked Mary about her glasses. Mary said, "Ja, he aimed a belt at me and a buckle hit my glasses."

We spoke to Busi. She lives in another township in another city. She has two children. Her husband has been beating her for sixteen years. She feels very alone with her troubles. She told us, "The whole yard hears my screams. He says he will kill me one day, and I believe this. No one comes because they say it is trouble between husband and wife." Busi has tried leaving home. Every time he looks for her. And she keeps going back. Busi says, "He says he wants my money. I get very upset. But the funny thing is that I am still hanging around with this man."

As we spoke to these women we felt very angry. We felt angry that such things happen to women. We felt angry because this beating of women is hidden away. It is a hidden crime. We felt angry because it is an accepted crime. Thousands of women live with battered faces and bruised bodies. Trying to hide what their men do to them. Trying to hide the hurt inside them as well. Isn't it time that women broke the silence about this crime?

So what kind of man beats his wife or girlfriend? The answer is – all kinds of men. Rich men, workers, unemployed men, white men and black men ... educated men and uneducated men ... old men and young men. All kinds of normal everyday men beat their wives. We have met women who are married to comrades who beat them. And we have met many women who say they don't want to marry. Many women say, "Who wants to be treated like a dog?"

We spoke to women from an organisation called People Opposed to Women Abuse (POWA). POWA helps women who have been beaten. They said, "We find the women feel very alone. They live inside themselves. This beating may have happened for years and years. It is important that the victims know it happens to many other women. It happens because men are trying to tell women that they are in control." POWA says that they want to help women get control over their lives.

But women's feelings about themselves and what they are worth also get a terrible beating. And sometimes that hurt inside lasts forever. Children learn from their parents. Men who beat their wives are teaching their sons to become batterers. And women who put up with it are teaching their daughters to put up with it.

Whey do women accept this life? Most women struggle to find an answer to this question. Some say there is a tradition that women must stay with their husbands. Also, many women rely on their husbands for money. Others say, "We have nowhere to go. The townships are already overcrowded." And even if a woman can find a place to stay, it is not easy to start a new life. And for some women not everything about the man is bad. There is some love – and a hope that the beatings will stop. And after years of beating, women start to believe that they are worth nothing. They feel guilty. They start to believe that they have done something to deserve the beating. It seems like a trap with no escape.

All women can do something about this problem. An injury to one is an injury to all. Women can help each other by talking about the problem. We can also do practical things – like giving someone who is running away from a beating a place to stay. We can help with looking after children.

This beating will not stop until women break their silence. It will not stop until men treat women as equals. It will not stop until women come together to organise to end this violence. Woman-beating must be taken up as an issue in all organisations.

SPEAK 20, 1988
Breaking the silence

Going around with SPEAK 19 was much more interesting than usual. Just about everyone we met had something to say about the article on woman-beating.

Some liked the article very much. They said: "It tells exactly what women go through", "It's very strong and has ideas of what women can do", "It was wonderful".

But others could not believe we were writing about such things. And these were mostly men. One man asked, "What are you saying? I have seen so many women beating men, but you say nothing about that." Another man said, "These things should be discussed in the bedroom." Yet another response was, "I don't believe it – you are asking women to form vigilante groups."

We decided to find out more about what people thought. Some students helped us. They took copies of SPEAK 19 to men and women and asked them to read the article. Later they went back for a chat. Only two of the people they spoke to said that men should beat their wives and girlfriends. These two felt that it was important that men showed who was the boss in the home. They also believed that it was tradition for men to show women their strength.

But most of the people we met said beating women was wrong and should be stopped. One young man said, "What you are asking me, sister, is if I was happy when my father beat up my mother. All this never made sense to me. My mother is not a child. My dad beat her up for things like not being home by 6 p.m. This only stopped the day my two brothers and I dealt with my father man-to-man."

Another man, a 45-year-old teacher, said, "It is true that it happens worldwide that women are beaten and even killed by their husbands. Only women can come together and fight this, because they are the ones who feel the pinch." This man had beaten his wife two weeks previously. He promised not to do it again and he took the magazine for his wife to read.

One woman thought beating was not right, but she saw it as part of life. She said, "My child, this is normal in our lives. People think there is something wrong with the woman rather than with the husband. That is why most of us stand it." Another woman said, "It is high time women fight for their rights. If two people do not agree they must talk together. There is no need for beatings."

It was good that people were willing to talk about this situation and that most wanted it to change. Let us fight to take these problems out of the bedroom so that we can work for a world where women are respected.

Graphic: Shamim

SPEAK 29, 1990

No to rape – Soweto women march against rape

"Joyina! Joyina! Join us! Join us! Stop rape in our township. We don't want it. Join us! It could be you next, it could be your daughter or mother next. It could be my daughter next. Join us! Let us stop these terrible rapes that happen." This is what Soweto women called out as they marched along the streets of Diepkloof, Soweto in February this year.

The anti-rape march was organised by church women. One of the organisers of the march, Maggie Nkwe, explained why they organised the march. She said: "One day in church at a prayer, one woman stood up and prayed for her granddaughter who had been raped. Another woman stood up and prayed for someone she knew who had been raped. Then another, and another, and another. Then we realised that this was an issue we had to take up. These rapes must stop."

Police say that in 1987 there were 1 947 rapes reported to police in Soweto. In 1989 there were 2 178 reported rapes. But these numbers do not tell the whole story. Not all women who are raped report the rape. It is estimated that in South Africa only one out of every 20 rapes is reported. Looking at figures for the country as a whole, it is estimated that 320 000 women are raped each year. In other words, every minute and a half a woman in South Africa is raped.

Rape is on the increase. And organised gang rape is also on the increase. In Soweto a gang called the "Jackrollers" has put more fear into women's lives. The more violent our society becomes, the more violence there is against women. Violence such as rape, battery and sexual harassment.

The Soweto women made history. It was one of the first times a march against rape was organised in our country. It was a march with a strong message. The march started small, but more and more people joined in along the way. By the end of the march more than 200 women had joined in. At first some passers-by thought the march was about the unbanning of the people's organisations that had taken place the day before.

But the placards told the message about the march. Placards spoke out about the problem of gang rapists and the terrible effect of rape on women. "Sexual abuse is a crime against humanity," said one placard. "There is no love in rape," said another.

Representatives of different organisations were on the march. Church women and women from the Federation of Transvaal Women and from People Opposing Women Abuse were there. Women from POWA spoke to us about the work they do: "POWA gives talks and workshops to raise awareness about rape. We also offer a counselling service for women. POWA gives emotional support and medical and legal advice to women who have been raped or battered. POWA runs a shelter where we give accommodation to women who are trying to leave a violent relationship. We offer a phone-in service to women needing help."

POWA spoke about why rape happens. "We believe that rape is a form of violence that men use on women. Men cause the violence because of the power they have over women in society."

People often believe that the women who get raped were to blame. They believe that women could have avoided it in some way. The women from POWA told us: "These false beliefs or 'myths' about rape are what we fight. Some of the myths are that women enjoy rape, that nice girls don't get raped, or that women ask to be raped by the way they dress. And there is the belief that only young women get raped. But this is all nonsense. Women of all ages get raped. Recently a four-year-old girl was raped by a stranger who broke in while the family was asleep. We cannot say that she asked to be raped, or that she was dressed to invite rape. We have to stop looking to females as the cause of rape. Men who rape are the ones to blame."

The women from POWA say, "Society teaches us that men and women should be treated differently. Boys are brought up to be strong, aggressive and in control of their lives. Many men do not think it is wrong to rape a woman. They think they have the right to take her, with force if necessary, when she does not agree."

POWA believes this violence can be stopped: "We have to educate people about the problem. We have to talk about the suffering it causes women. People must learn that sexism oppresses women. The fear of violence oppresses women. Women's voices must be strong. So that liberation in South Africa will also mean liberation from rape, battery, sexual harassment and the fear of violence."

POWA believes progressive organisations have a role to play in ending rape and violence against women. "It is up to people's organisations to change attitudes in our society. The ideas people have about rape, sexism, women's exploitation and abuse have to be challenged. These issues must be raised in organisations. Most organisations state in their constitutions that they are against sexism, but issues affecting women are not taken seriously. The issue of violence and abuse of women should be put high on the agenda of progressive organisations, and there should be more education on women's issues. Rape and women-abuse should be fought as seriously as racism is fought. Only in this way can we hope to end rape.

"The struggle to end violence against women is linked to the struggle for liberation from racism, oppression and exploitation in this country. It must be understood that violence against women is part of the violence that is increasing in our country right now. Violence has become a way of life. It has become a weapon of those who have power against those who do not have it. The liberation of women is fundamental to the liberation of all oppressed in South Africa."

Rape is a serious crime. A girl or woman who is raped lives with the terrible memory of it all her life. In many cases rape has led to the death of the women who are raped.

A fifteen-year-old who was raped by gangsters recently died at the Hillbrow Hospital. She fell pregnant as a result of the rape and she died after having a legal abortion. Her mother said that the daughter was so badly affected by the rape she would kill herself rather than have the baby.

SPEAK dedicates this article to that young Sowetan woman and to all the thousands of girls and women who have suffered the terrible trauma of rape. Women must unite to fight the violence that affects them. A new South Africa must protect women from abuse against them. And the fight for that new South Africa must begin now!

Soweto church women march against rape in February 1990.   *Photo: Gille, You and Me Images*

A marriage of blood and beatings

Thirty-four-year-old Helen Smith (not her real name) stayed in a violent marriage for ten years. Eventually she went for help to the Eldorado Park Violence Prevention Programme – an advice centre for battered women. She tells her story.

"A few weeks after getting married my husband Joseph started to beat me. The beatings got so bad I ended up in hospital. From that time on, the hospital staff saw more of me than the shopkeeper.

"I do not remember a single happy moment in my ten years of marriage to Joseph. What I do remember is being beaten, sworn at and humiliated. My husband drank a lot and was a drug addict. Even when I was pregnant he beat me. With my second pregnancy my baby stopped growing inside me. I thought I was going to lose it.

"I left Joseph a few times, but I always went back to him – I don't know why. I know it wasn't for love. He is the father of my children and I did not want to break up the family.

"I tried to kill myself many times. I drank paraffin, took tablet overdoses, tried to cut myself … I can't even remember what else.

"Because of the beatings I am blind in one eye. I have stab wounds all over my body. My bowel is not working properly. My face has been damaged and I get headaches all the time. It all became too much. I heard of the Eldorado Park Violence Prevention Programme from a nurse, and I visited the centre. But when Joseph found out he beat me up again. I recently decided to divorce him. Lawyers told me to give it another try. I did.

"Two days later Joseph cut open my stomach with a knife. I had to hold my intestines in my hand on the way to the hospital.

"I have left him now. This time, forever. I am staying in a shelter for abused women, trying to get my life together. There are many scars I will never be able to get rid of, but I know I will end up in the mortuary if I go back to him again."

Rape is a crime of violence *by Claire Keeton*

Every day there are at least four rape cases in the magistrate's court in Mdantsane, Ciskei. Often, though, it is the woman who seems to be on trial. Claire Keeton went to one of the cases.

Nomsa (not her real name) stands in the witness box with clenched fists. The thirteen-year-old schoolgirl looks straight ahead and tells the court how she was raped. She describes the attack with surprising calm.

She was coming back from the bus stop one evening when she saw two boys near the church. One went away and the other pulled her along by her arm to a deserted bushy area. Nomsa told him to leave her. She screamed and he took off his jersey to close her mouth. He got on top of her.

"He took out a knife from his pocket and said if I don't take off my panties he will stab me. I refused. He cut me on my thigh and pulled up my skirt. He pulled down my panties and threw them far away. He opened my thighs roughly and then he raped me," Nomsa tells the court.

"Then he heard people talking and he said I should keep quiet. I did not, I cried. Then Bra Mzi saw him and asked him what he was doing. He ran away and Bra Mzi found me on the ground."

Madoda Dyonana, the boy accused of raping Nomsa, says she is his girlfriend. He claims she loves him and agreed to have sex. He tells the court that he proposed love to her at a children's party a few weeks earlier, and she accepted. He says they held hands. Nomsa denies this, but Dyonana's best friend supports him. He says it was clear that the two had a relationship.

The senior prosecutor accuses Dyonana and his friend of lying. One of the first questions he asks Nomsa is whether she had an affair with Dyonana. "No," she says without hesitating. Asked if the sex was painful, Nomsa says yes.

The magistrate finds Dyonana guilty of rape. He sentences him to three years in prison because he is still young.

Later that day Nomsa is back at school. Her mother says Nomsa is glad the court found Dyonana guilty. "She was so shocked after the rape, she was dizzy and did not sleep so well," says Nomsa's mother. "She was afraid of that man. Yes, he should go to prison."

SPEAK 55, 1993

Alone in their silence – not any more *by Rosalee Telela*

Suzette Mafuna is a woman who was abused by her husband for a long time. She lived with the abuse until, one day, he nearly killed her. She left him. This is her story.

"I survived the abuse, but healing from the scars and the pain never ends. It is still difficult for me to trust any man who wants to get close to me. I'm so scared of the same thing happening all over again. I still have nightmares. It was not easy for me to leave my husband, I was scared of what he might do to me.

"There were many reasons why I stayed in my marriage. I felt pity for my husband. Every time he said, 'I'm sorry, please forgive me. I love you,' I felt sorry for him. I also did not want to believe that he was a violent person. Because I loved him so much, I'd simply forgive him and try to love him even more. The love slowly began to die. And for my own sake, I knew I had to get out.

"My family and friends also put a lot of pressure on me. I used to run home to my mother when he abused me. My mother would tell me that a woman is supposed to handle these things. I started to believe that I was not good enough and that I deserved what was happening to me. Later, I got a lot of support from women, friends and family. I was lucky. Women must see that it is not their fault if they are abused by their partners. They should not feel scared to speak about what's happening to them. It's the only way something can be done about their abuse."

BREAKING THE SILENCE

WOMEN SAY OUR MEN MUST STOP BEATING US

Graphic: Sanna

Many women have stopped taking this abuse. They have formed organisations that give support and counselling to women who have been raped, abused and beaten up. These organisations provide places of healing and safety, but they also add to the voices calling for and working for a change in men's attitudes towards women. According to Belinda Martin of Women Against Women Abuse (WAWA), Eldorado Park outside Johannesburg has a high number of battery, rape and abuse cases. WAWA gives safety and support to women in Eldorado Park who are in abusive relationships. Martin says: "It is important that a woman who has come out in the open about her abusive relationship feels safe with the person she talks to. She must know she is speaking to someone who believes her and wants to help her."

Many of these organisations have shelters that serve as places of safety and support. "The first place a woman who is abused needs is a place of safety. Family and friends are often too afraid to help because they are scared of the abuser. The woman finds herself running around with nowhere to go. The shelter is a place of safety for the woman where she can begin to recover from the pain," says Martin. "With the shelters and counselling, women will become strong and will see their strength, a strength which gets destroyed when they are abused by men."

Lisa Vetten of POWA said her organisation focuses on education as well. "We see education as a way to make people aware and to put pressure on the government, hospitals and the police to change their attitudes towards women who are abused."

She believes one of the reasons for the violence women face is that society does not value women as highly as it values men.

SPEAK 66, 1994
Love shouldn't hurt *by Rosalee Telela*

She is slapped, punched, sworn at, kicked, raped, strangled, burnt. She bruises, loses an eye, a kidney, an unborn baby, her confidence. Maybe even her life. Brutality against women in our society is real. Frightening, real, very common and mostly ignored.

Agisanang Domestic Abuse Prevention and Training (ADAPT) deals with this brutality every day. You will find ADAPT inside the brightly coloured walls of Alexandra clinic, in Alexandra township. There a very special woman, Mmatshilo Motsei, deals with the painful reality of violence against women. She is the project's founder.

Outspoken, confident, courageous, Mmatshilo is herself a survivor of violent abuse. An organiser for change. How did it all begin?

When the beatings began, Mmatshilo was depressed and confused. She even thought of committing suicide. "The pain becomes so much that you can't go on. I understand when women in violent relationships are confused. One day they decide to leave the abuser, the next day they don't.

"But we don't have to be hard on ourselves. There are too many people battering us. We don't have to do it to ourselves. We need to be gentle with ourselves and support each other, as women."

Although she believes women can nurture and love each other, they do not always support one another. "When I decided to leave, my mother supported my decision. Unfortunately for most women in our community, their mothers tell them to go back, even if their husbands beat them up daily. They say we received lobola from these people, and, as a wife, you should withstand all the problems that come with being married."

Motsei says there are traditional ways of dealing with marital problems such as wife-abuse. Unfortunately, these do not take into account what the woman thinks or feels. "After your family and his family have sat down and talked about the problems, most of the time you're just told to go back to your partner. He continues to abuse you, knowing that even if you go home, another 'indaba' will be called, and you will be sent back to him."

Motsei believes men's violent behaviour has a lot to do with the history of this country and how respect and pride have broken down. "The violence that comes with racism and poverty has pushed people to do things they wouldn't normally do." However, Motsei says poverty is not the main cause of violence against women. "Men learn from an early age to see and treat women as objects. They have been raised to believe that a real man is one who is able to control women by being aggressive and violent."

South African structures, institutions, cultures and practices (which are male-dominated) justify, maintain and reproduce violence. "When a woman goes to a religious leader for advice, she is told to love, honour, obey and suffer in silence. Sometimes we are even told it is our fault that men abuse us. I know of a priest in Soweto who tells the women who go to see him, 'If your husband beats you, it's a cross you should carry, like Jesus Christ.'"

Motsei says the use of scriptures to justify violence is only one side of the story. "Those priests do not mention that in the same chapter they quote, there is a request for men to respect and love women as they would love their own bodies." She also believes it is not the will of God that women should live with violence. "I think God would expect us to speak out against violence, and do something about it."

A closer look at history tells how violence against women was discouraged in the past. "Long ago, in most African cultures, when you got married, one of the things said to a man was, 'If you don't want her anymore, you must bring her back. Don't hurt her.'"

Although most health workers are women, most cases of women-abuse are not reported, says Motsei. "Many nurses have experienced violence in their lives. When they come across a woman who has been battered or raped, it's something they find hard to deal with." This is one of the reasons why ADAPT was set up. To run workshops on how to identify abuse and offer help. Also, to offer counselling and support to abused women.

Motsei says women need to make their voices heard. They have to stop taking the blame and stop feeling ashamed. "This is where the role of women's groups, associations, stokvels and prayer meetings come in. Women are organised in so many ways. They have to start discussing issues like rape, abuse and abortion. If a few women speak out, others are going to follow.

"If there is a death in your area where a woman has been killed by her husband, make a noise about it. Expose the man who did it."

The constitution, the Bill of Rights, the Criminal Procedure Act and the Prevention of Family Violence Act say violence against women is a crime. However, laws alone are not enough. Attitudes have to change. Police, courts, hospitals, clinics, schools and social workers also have to start seeing women-abuse as a crime. And, of course, so do the abusers.

"Men have got to take responsibility for their violence. They need to challenge all the lies they have been told about women. They have to look closely at how they have been raised, because these things are learned early in life. It starts with the games boys and girls play."

Motsei has some ideas about getting men to take responsibility. "I think we do have men who are our allies. Men who condemn gender violence as strongly as we do. Those men could be trained as counsellors for abusive men. They can be role models for others. To say to men it's okay not to be violent – that it does not make you less of a man."

Motsei believes men who abuse should, however, be punished. "The sentences given for violent crimes against women have to be harsh. When a man beats or rapes a woman it should be seen as a serious crime. At the moment men do it because they can get away with it. There is no message coming from society saying it is wrong."

Graphic: Mannik Design

Struggles Today

An interview with one of the organisations in the National Network Against Violence Against Women – NISAA Institute for Women's Development – highlights some of the work being done today. NISAA was started at the end of 1993 in Lenasia, a township set up under apartheid for Indian South Africans. NISAA offers counselling, a shelter and opportunities for women's empowerment. Zubeida Dangor, a founder and the co-ordinator of NISAA, spoke in April 1997 of the work they are doing.

Zubeida said: "NISAA is an Arabic word for women. NISAA was formally launched in March 1994 by a group of gender activists. We had a clear decision to establish a shelter for women who were abused. Together with that we have a focus on women's rights relating to violence. We started with a process of training, preventative education and then we set up a shelter.

"The organisation is based in Lenasia and is open to everybody. As it is close to Soweto and close to taxis and the railway, 80% of our clients are from Soweto. We also have clients from Lenasia, Eldorado Park and Ennerdale.

"We offer a short-term crisis shelter. A 24-hour service where women can call if battered or if their lives are endangered. Women receive counselling for between four to six weeks."

In addition to counselling, NISAA offers skills training which can lead to greater economic independence. "We help women to define goals. We offer skills training, for example in computers, developing vegetable gardens, etc." Often resources of other organisations are drawn on in order to provide the necessary training. "We access resources we know of or can find. At times we pay for training. At times we link with the Department of Manpower who offer training, or we try to get work done by agencies in the community."

Zubeida tells how NISAA was formed. "I am a trained psychologist. I saw more and more women with depression. I found a lot of abuse in their lives. There were no resources, nowhere to go except POWA. I worked at Coronation hospital, at the Family Life Centre in Lenasia and in Eldorado Park. On the basis on my experience I ran a workshop in 1989. We felt we had to look at how to set up resources. I spent six months in the USA visiting shelters."

Dangor points out that shelters for women are an important resource since women's lives are often endangered. At the same time, however, preventative work is also important. NISAA works in schools on a violence prevention programme, which offers assertiveness and problem-solving skills training. NISAA also trains nurses, paramedics and other groups within the community who would potentially see women.

Some of the women who have been in the shelter are employed at NISAA. "Two ex-residents run the shelter," says Dangor. "This is a powerful example of how the shelter can be run with their experiences."

In 1996/1997 NISAA launched the "White Ribbon Campaign" together with the Gauteng Network Against Violence Against Women. NISAA produced information pamphlets in English, Zulu and Sotho. These were given to various organisations, which were asked to organise talks in their constituencies. Many organisations which would not ordinarily have dealt with this issue became involved in the campaign.

The national network has taken up the issue of violence against women with various government ministers and departments. The network launched a police training programme, which has been going on for about a year. One hundred police officers are trained a month. This process is being monitored as a pilot.

Dangor believes violence against women is a societal problem, with its roots in the power and control society gives men over women. She believes this can be changed, however. She reminds us that although this seems an impossible task, we need to remember the struggle against apartheid. We could have had a similar view of apartheid, which seemed at the time to be a system we could not crush. "It depends on our vision," she says. The struggle for an end to violence requires "changing the attitudes of men and women. The root cause of violence needs to be treated."

As a result of its work, NISAA does get attacked openly. But, says Dangor, "The more the resistance, the more we see women taking up their rights."

YOU CAN'T STOP THE SPIRIT

You can't stop the spirit
She is like the mountains
Old and strong
She'll go on
and on
and on
You can't kill the spirit

95

CHAPTER FOUR

The Personal is Political

When we started SPEAK, we often heard comments that ideas of women's liberation were foreign to African tradition and culture. That these ideas were Western and bourgeois, and had nothing to do with the struggles of black, working-class women in South Africa. But the more we talked and listened to women in communities and factories, the more this was proved wrong.

Whenever women came together it was clear that it was these very personal struggles that held us back. Women in communities talked in their women's groups about difficulties in getting to meetings because of husbands who expected meals on time. Women in trade unions talked of similar problems. Women's time was not their own time. They were expected to spend it in endless work and they needed their men's permission before they could make decisions about what to do and where to go. Trade-union women raised issues such as sharing housework and child care with men, sexual harassment from male comrades and the traditional attitudes of men and women. Women talked about violence in the form of rape and beatings by men.

Women spent a lot of time talking about such personal problems because these are important. They overcame the difficulties of speaking about these matters because they realised things needed to change. It is not easy to speak out about these personal struggles because we were told they were not important – that the liberation struggle should come first. That we should unite with our men against the common enemy of apartheid. That a good woman is one who enjoys serving her family, who is submissive and loyal. It took a lot of courage to talk about the personal struggles in women's lives.

In the articles in this chapter women question the unquestionable. They challenge age-old customs, such as lobola and polygamy. A woman who does not want to be a mother speaks out against the pressures on women to have children. A single mother tells of her struggles in a community where choosing to be single is not an easy choice to live out. One woman tells of how she walked out on her boyfriend in the middle of the night, because she could not bear to continue a relationship which meant sexual satisfaction for him but not for her.

Women bus drivers and women priests talk of their struggles for acceptance in male-dominated areas. Lesbian women reveal their struggles in letting their families and the world know that they are lesbian – and the struggle of even admitting this to themselves. They speak of the violence they suffer. And they talk of the second-class status they have within gay organisations which are dominated by gay men.

Finally, women and men talk of the problem of the abortion laws under apartheid. Not being able to get legal abortions meant that many women were forced to have back-street operations, often leading to complications and even deaths.

All these struggles are very personal, and women are expected to carry them as private burdens. But they are also political struggles. They affect almost all women, they limit women's opportunities and life chances, and they are the result of the power men have over women in the world we live in.

As Thenjiwe Mtintso (presently ANC secretary general) says, the struggles women fight in their personal lives are important (SPEAK 56). She points out that for the sake of peace in the home, many strong women choose to wash the dishes and ignore the oppression they face in their homes. But, in fact, it is this struggle which is central to our daily lives and liberation.

In the new South Africa all these issues continue to be relevant if women are to have control over their own lives. These struggles demand changes in our own attitudes, the attitudes of our families, and the attitudes of the men we live with and love. This is perhaps the hardest of all struggles.

Of all these "personal and political" issues, women have acted most strongly in the 1990s against violence against women and the right to abortion. Two key networks that have spearheaded these struggles are the Violence Network and the Reproductive Rights Network.

The one main victory women have won in the new South Africa is the changes in the abortion law. In 1997 a new law, the Choice on Termination of Pregnancy Act, was passed, allowing women to end pregnancies if they so chose. This is a victory for women's rights and brings to an end back-street deaths as the only option for women who do not want to continue a pregnancy.

It is going to take some time before the government puts the resources in place which are necessary to implement the law. These include human resources, training, equipment, facilities and drugs. In the meantime, women have been able to get terminations done at the Marie Stopes clinics, which could perform terminations in 1997 at a cost of between R400 and R800, depending on the location of the clinic. There are Marie Stopes clinics in Bloemfontein, Cape Town, Durban, Johannesburg, Randburg, Port Elizabeth and Soweto at present. Two more are planned for Nelspruit and Pretoria.

SPEAK 8, 1985

Ana's story – One woman's personal account

I won't forget what has happened in my life. I haven't got a husband because my husband died in Johannesburg. After that I met a man with no wife. I stayed together with him in KwaMashu with his children and his grandchild. But he didn't like my children, saying they finish the food. He refused to have them written in the file for the house and to get them a permit.

I stayed being worried about my children. He called my children snakes. He said to me, "I won't grow these snakes which are going to hit me tomorrow."

One day when I was at work one of the women told me about the Lindelani squatter camp. Then the following Saturday we went there and I got a site for myself. The following Sunday I bought some building materials at Microl Timbers. I haven't got money to buy corrugated iron so I have to stay in this little house of boards.

One night the rains came and the water got into the house. I had to get up to dig drains inside my house so that the water must go out. The side of the house came off and the roof was off with the wind. And now it's still like that because I am trying to buy stuff to build a roof. The sides of the house I will make from mud. Every Saturday and Sunday I do this work.

SPEAK 20, 1988

Another kind of life

Think of a day when you come home from work and somebody else is seeing to the children, making sure that they get ready to sleep, making sure that the older ones are doing their homework. Is this kind of life just a dream?

Think of a time when you finish cooking and sit down while somebody else is cleaning up, and you also get a chance to relax with your children. Think of a moment when the man in you life agrees that you need rest, that you need to go out and be away from the housework – or that you need to attend a meeting without feeling guilty about child care and other responsibilities at home.

It was hard to find families like this. Not many men know that it takes sharing to make a relationship enjoyable. But there were signs of hope.

Ndumiso is not married. He lives with his mother, brothers and sisters. He said, "I don't mind doing work in the house. As long as it needs to be done, I do it. After all, we share the house – why can't we share the housework as well?"

Often the reason men don't want to work in the home is the fear of what people are going to say about them. Magrapes and Thabo are two men who have had this problem. Magrapes shares the housework with his wife. He told us, "One day I was

doing washing for the family outside the house. Another man just came angrily and spoke to me. He complained that I was setting a bad example. He said now all the women around will expect men to wash for them."

This way of thinking comes from the way we are brought up. We are told that a good wife is one who does everything for a man. We forget that sharing housework means both a man and a woman will have more time together at the end of the day. It also means that love will grow.

Thabo is married and has children. "I wash nappies for my little ones whenever I can. But I know that people think that it is the worst thing for a man to look after children. My neighbour started singing a song saying that my wife was bossy. I ignored him. I told my wife and we both laughed about it."

Brian looks after his two children. He said, "Men live only half-lives until they care for their children. Looking after children is a joy. It makes you a full human being. Your children don't know you and you don't know them until you look after them."

Ndumiso is a member of a community organisation that is fighting for change so that people can live better lives. He said, "For me, democracy applies from the time I wake up in the morning, at the workplace and in my organisation." Ndumiso feels strongly that male comrades must make sure that the women in their lives have the time to get involved in community and union struggles. He said it's a mistake for men in the struggle to leave their wives out of what they are doing. "You need that support from each other in order to grow."

We also spoke to women about this problem. There were very few women who found men willing to share everything. One woman said, "It's very nice to be in a relationship where everything is shared. You get to love and understand each other better. But it is a big battle. It does not happen overnight. You have to keep reminding the man you live with that you are also a human being. But it need not get to the point of quarrelling; if a person is loving, then he should understand your concern."

Graphic: SPEAK

Another woman said, "We are facing many problems. There are laws which make it difficult for people to have normal lives. Workers are fighting for better conditions, people are dying in the townships every day. Many people feel that talking about problems between men and women these days is just crazy. They believe that fighting bosses and the government for our rights is the only battle. But, if we win the bigger fight, will women be free?"

SPEAK 25, 1989
Is lobola still worthwhile?

SPEAK went out and asked young people what they thought of lobola, or bride price, in these changing times. The question we asked was: "Will there be lobola in a post-apartheid South Africa?" The people we asked had a lot to say.

Some saw lobola as a good part of our cultural heritage and others saw it as oppressive to women. Some said that the meaning and value of lobola had changed over the years.

Palesa Xorile, a 23-year-old student from Soweto, said, "Because lobola is our culture, and it was there before the emergence of Western culture, it should exist in a post-apartheid South Africa. Our great-grandparents valued lobola because it shows the pride the parents have in their daughter."

Tumi Manbena is a 20-year-old student. He felt there would not be lobola in the future because it has lost its value. He said, "There is no difference because young people stay together without lobola. Especially in the urban areas. The generation of today are less interested in tradition."

Evelyn Lehoki, a 20-year-old student, feels strongly about the subject: "In a post-apartheid society we will be guided by an ideal of a non-racial democratic South Africa. So there will be no prejudice on mixed marriages. Therefore we will have to achieve a common culture across the colour line. I believe there will be new norms to replace the marriage negotiations."

Some people believe that if you do not pay lobola you do not value the woman. Others say that lobola has turned into a business. Others say that lobola turns women into things you can buy, like furniture. Nineteen-year-old Nomvula Toko said, "Lobola restores family pride in the bride. The groom shows the bride's family that he will be able to take care of their daughter since he is able to pay lobola. Lobola is not a trade, but an acceptance of two families, a way to bring the two families together."

Aaron Matlala disagrees. "The money paid for lobola brings inequality between men and women, because the man will regard his wife as a commodity. He is going to control his wife whenever he wants. And the woman must not say anything because the woman was paid for. If lobola does not exist, there will be a contract between men and women that will show the two are married. In that way men and women will be equal and they will share everything equally."

Nana Gumede, who is 35 years old, refuses to accept that the lobola system is in any way good for women. She said, "Parents demand thousands of rands for their daughter. They don't think of the financial problems they are putting on the young couple. And then once lobola has been paid he expects the wife to jump when he tells her to. I' m not interested in lobola. My father knows this and we argue about it. But I say that if he demands five thousand rand, I will pay half and my husband will pay half. There is no way I will be paid for."

SPEAK 36, 1991

As proud as a peacock: A true story

After having sex one night I said to him: "Ai, have you finished?"

He said: "Yes"

I said: "Are you happy?"

He said: "Why?"

I said: "I am just asking because I feel that you are only interested in yourself."

He became angry, and as he became angry I became angry. Eventually he cooled off and went to sleep. But I remained angry seeing how he was feeling nice and relaxed after sex, leaving me on the other side. I couldn't sleep. I told myself this is one thing I could not allow to happen again. I knew when he woke up he may want sex again. I would rather go home than sleep with him again just to satisfy him.

It was after twelve at night, and dark. When I got outside I hesitated, but I told myself I could not sleep. I saw a car coming and I waved. He flashed past, but he came back. Yes, I was taking a risk, but I felt I could not continue in my boyfriend's house. If he felt there was something wrong he would have listened when I talked to him about it. But he didn't.

I loved my boyfriend very much, and I had been with him for quite some time. He was a gentleman and very handsome. But this problem was something I could not take.

The driver of the car opened the window and asked why I was out there at that time of night. I told him I had a problem and I asked if he could take me to the taxi terminus in Johannesburg. He said it was late – he didn't want to pass by the following morning and see a dead woman lying by the road.

In the end he took me home. On my way from Alexandra to Soweto I started to cool off. I started to discuss it with him. I said, "It's what you people are doing to us." He even slowed down to listen to what I was saying. He said he didn't know it hurt women when men behaved like that. He said he thought having sex was just to please one person – the man. He said that women didn't ever complain about it. He dropped me right at my gate. I thanked him and I went in. I had given him something to think about.

The next morning I felt proud of what I had done. I had not kept quiet about the problem. I asked my women colleagues how they felt about this whole thing. They said, "You are telling the truth. We have this problem and we are not in a position to voice it, because if you say something you will be called names. Women are only in love to satisfy, not to be satisfied."

My boyfriend was very sorry for his attitude. But I could not forgive him. He should have done something at the time. Instead he said, "I am tired, I want to go to sleep." That is the attitude we get from men.

These things need to be discussed openly, because they affect the relationship between two people. Because men are dominant they think they can do whatever they like, whenever they like. Even if a man is married he can divorce you today and get married tomorrow. He can go out and propose love to any woman he likes. If a man sees a pretty woman he will want to sleep with her. But a woman who sees a handsome man doesn't just want to sleep with him. She wants to know him better.

I've seen that nowadays our women have started to realise that men are doing a wrong thing. Many women even feel they would rather stay without a boyfriend than stay with men who don't show they care.

I left my boyfriend. I'm one person who doesn't like to be messed up. And I don't like messing other people up. I made an impact on him, and he keeps reminding me of this. He says openly that I taught him a lesson. In fact he says he wants to marry me. But I say, "No ways". I would prefer to go to the next one and teach him, rather than teach this one who knows. I felt great that at long last I had voiced my problem ... I felt proud as a peacock.

SPEAK 39, 1992

The cutting edge *by Mahadi Miya*

More and more people are choosing not to get married these days. This isn't always an easy choice. Mahadi Miya writes that society still looks down on singles:

As a single, independent person I have been harassed by my family, my neighbours and society in general. Single people – especially women – are not treated as capable, honourable human beings. It is definitely taking people too long to catch up with the singles and their lifestyles.

My first bad experience was with my family. They felt I had disgraced them by falling pregnant out of marriage. They were even more furious when I refused to marry the father of my child. I was made to feel stupid and unreasonable. Nobody cared to find out my reasons. I was just told it was not decent to be an unmarried parent.

This just made me even more determined to do what I knew was right for me and my daughter. I could not marry a man who was not prepared to share the simple things like baby-sitting, nappy changing and child-care expenses.

Talking about expenses, it is not easy to cope financially as a single mother. Now and then I find myself spending money unnecessarily, for a toy or a sweet-looking outfit. As my daughter has got older it has become more difficult. She demands this and that because she sees it on other kids. I don't want her to feel that she is worse-off because of my decision to stay single. But it digs a hole in my pocket.

Then a year ago I had to face the world. I decided to buy myself a house and move out of my mother's home. I took my daughter with me. My family by now had learnt that they couldn't give me orders.

It wasn't easy to make the move. I was lucky my friends supported me. Since deciding to move, I have had to face all kinds of male harassment. It has been far worse than ever before. There was a lot of paperwork associated with the move. Whenever I got to any office where I was served by men, they never failed to tell me about their wishes to know me better. I felt that my single status was a threat to these men. The word "Mrs" before one's name is obviously still some barrier against male harassment. The word "Miss" makes them think one is available.

Graphic:
Adapted by Shamim

After the move I had to face my new neighbours. As soon as they noticed I was without a man or a "Mrs" before my name they started feeling that maybe I was an enemy. They seemed to feel they couldn't trust me. In the beginning there was a sudden interest from the men. They started to visit me without their wives. I soon managed to make it clear to them I was not stranded. I had chosen to be single.

The women ignored me. They would not ask me to join in any of the neighbourhood activities like planning for block funerals. I did not let it bother me. I kept to myself and ignored them. Then after a few weeks in my new house I woke up one morning to find my back-yard fence standing open. Somebody had cut it. I could see that it was done very neatly, and probably by an adult.

I decided to get the fence fixed and not worry about it. Alas! Two weeks later it was cut again in the same spot as the first time. This time I decided to leave it standing open. I wanted to show them I didn't care.

All I know is that my backyard fence would be standing whole if I had a pair of trousers as window dressing!

SPEAK 43, 1992
Preassure to bear children *by Nana Gumede*

Society puts too much pressure on women to have children. So writes Nana Gumede, who doesn't want to be a mother:

So much for our "right to chose". Try explaining to your family and friends that you have chosen not to have children.

You have had it! Everyone looks at you as if you are mad and an embarrassment to the family. "How can you go against nature?" they ask. "How can you deprive your mother of holding the little bundle of joy in her arms?" They tell you of this great miracle – the birth experience – and how it is something only women can go through. You are told of this great love you will feel and how empty your life is, has been and will be until you have gone through childbirth. Friends come up with all sorts of stories to help you change your mind. They tell you how your life will change on the arrival of this little person.

All this is said by the very people who have complained about the pain of childbirth, sleepless nights, midnight feeds, dirty nappies – not forgetting useless partners who sleep through all of this!

Well, to every one of them I say, "To each his own poison."

Having seen some examples of these "bundles of joy" I prefer to call them "bundles of woe". I made my decision not to have children more than 20 years ago. It is a carefully thought-out decision. It is not because I do not like children. It is just that I do not choose to have any of my own. I choose to sleep peacefully without having to wake up to entertain someone else. I choose to think for myself, and of myself first. I choose to be myself, and not someone else's mom.

It is time society accepts and lives with the fact that people have different lifestyles. A woman should have the right to be called child-free and not childless – as if there is something lacking in her because she does not have a child. The right to choose should rest with every person.

SPEAK 44, 1992
Women behind the wheel *by Hassen Lorgat*

Don't you kill us! Can you drive? These are some of the things passengers say when they see a woman driving a bus. SPEAK asked two bus drivers about their work. Jenny Solomon and Rachma Kubie were among the first women to be employed as bus drivers by the Johannesburg Municipality Transport Department. Some men bus drivers were furious. They said, "What do you want here? You must go home and cook."

Passengers also found it hard to accept. Jenny remembers the days when her bus ran empty because "passengers were not sure of us women bus drivers". When they eventually began to get into the women's buses they would say things like "Don't kill us", "Can you drive?" and "This is a man's job."

Jenny laughs when Rachma describes her own experience. "When I first drove my bus down Fox Street, people were shocked. But that was not the end of it, because my bus was followed by Jenny in her bus. Two women bus drivers in a row – that was just too much for them!"

One of their favourite stories is Jenny's conversation with an old blind passenger.

Blind woman: "Is this bus going to Forest Hill?"

Jenny: "Yes, it is."

Blind woman: "Listen lady, I am not talking to you, I'm talking to the driver!"

Although Rachma and Jenny laugh and joke about their jobs, bus driving is hard work. They work odd hours and long shifts. Their wages are not great, so they often work overtime to make ends meet. They get backache and problems with sleeping because of shift work. This kind of work really affects family life. When Jenny got married her husband wanted her to leave work. She told him he married her as a bus driver – and that was the way things would stay. Jenny loves her work.

Rachma and her husband have a "first-come first-cook" policy – the one who gets home first does the cooking. Her husband also shares the work of cleaning the house.

Both Rachma and Jenny applied for their jobs because they were tired of working in offices and factories and wanted a challenge. The pay was also better. Asked what they like most about their jobs, Rachma and Jenny say they love meeting new people.

Now there are more women drivers, and men drivers are used to it. But it's mainly a man's job. Of the 520 bus drivers who work for the Johannesburg Municipality, only eleven are women.

WOMEN PRIESTS – At last! *by Nicola Coningsby*

In late 1992, after a long struggle, women were at last ordained as priests in the Anglican Church.

It was a rich and special day for all ... South Africa's first Anglican women priests were ordained in Grahamstown, Eastern Cape, in September this year. Three women – Professor Nancy Charlton, Dr Bride Dickson and Sue Groves – were ordained by the Right Reverend Russel, the Bishop of Grahamstown.

The decision that women could be ordained as priests was made by 79% of those who attended the Triennial Synod of the Anglican Church a few months previously. But this decision is not forced on all the dioceses. It is left up to individual bishops to decide whether or not to allow women priests in their diocese.

During the ceremony in Grahamstown there was a moment of tension when Bishop Russel asked if anyone had any reason why the ceremony should not go ahead – but no one stood up. Friends and relatives joined the ceremony by helping the newly ordained women priests put on their priestly robes.

The Dean of Grahamstown, the Very Reverend Anthony Mdletshe, said in his sermon that the church was standing between the dying old order and the new one. He quoted the American civil rights leader Martin Luther King, saying, "What we see today is a foretaste of things to come."

Newly ordained Professor Nancy Charlton said, "Jesus came to proclaim the Kingdom 2 000 years ago. Its taken 1 700 years to accept slavery wasn't part of the Christian dispensation and its taken 2 000 years to realise women are full human beings." She said the decision would make more women want to join the ministry. "Some women have held back because they didn't want to accept second-class citizenship in the Church. I accepted it seven years ago in obedience to Christ."

A big problem has been tradition. "Traditionally, people with authority are men. It's a culture shock for some to accept women as people of authority. But Jesus didn't take notice of tradition. He invited Mary to sit at his feet and learn the law when only men could be scholars."

When asked what, as a woman priest, she would be able to bring to the Church, she said, "Women have gifts which are different, but go together well with the gifts of men. The Church hasn't recognised their gifts, only letting them make tea and do housekeeping duties. In particular, women have the gift of caring and the Church hasn't recognised this gift."

Charlton said she felt sorry for those who had opposed the ordination of women. "I have experienced pain and rejection for sixteen years, but I haven't left the Church or made a song and dance about it. I know the pain they are experiencing and I pray for them."

Ai! These double standards

Different standards are expected from women and men in society – and women suffer because of it, says Desmond Missouw, a Khanya College student from Soweto.

It is worrying to hear men say they only want to marry virgins and women who do not have children. Men say, "Lo ya umtwana ugrand, indaba unengcosi – that lady is lovely, the only problem is she has a child."

Didn't that woman get the child through a man? The very man saying those words may well have a child or two outside marriage, or he could be a divorcee.

The same double standards go for virginity. Men want virgins, while they themselves are not virgins. Families make the problem worse by looking down on a man who marries a women who already has a child. They say: "Uyokondla abantwana benye indoda – he is going to maintain another man's child." The woman may be financially independent, although that is not the point. The very same family wants their daughter to get married even if she has "illegitimate" children. All the same, if she finds a man with no children there are fewer problems.

A man must always have the best, not "second-hand" women, as the saying goes. It is not so important if he himself is so-called second-hand.

Someone once said that a man treats women in the same way as a baboon behaves in a mielie field. The baboon goes into a mielie field to steal cobs and he starts at one end of the field, picks a cob and puts it under his armpit. The he moves on to the next one. When he lifts his arm to put the second one away, the first one drops to the ground.

This will go on until he reaches the end of the field. He will only have one cob under his armpit but a lot of damage has been left behind. There are mielie cobs scattered all over the field.

I can see my womanhood clearly *by Kate Truscott*

Shanaaz Majiet represents Disabled People South Africa in the Western Cape Women's National Coalition. She has just completed a law degree at the University of Cape Town.

"At the time of my accident I had just passed standard nine. I spent only three months in hospital: most people with my injuries spend at least eight months. But I was in a rush to get on with my life, so I went back to school. That year I failed matric and this was a big blow to me because I had always done well at school. It was hard to come to terms with failure. People asked me, 'Wouldn't you be better-off with your own kind in a disabled school?' I said, 'No way.' I swallowed my pride and went back to my old school. This was tough, but I persisted and passed.

"I am the eldest child and my parents are divorced, so I was used to having responsibilities. But after the accident the reaction of my family was confusing. We went through months of arguments. They wanted to do everything for me. The flat we lived in was very small and I couldn't get into the kitchen in my wheelchair. I thought I was the only one who had to adapt to the situation; I didn't realise my family had to adapt too. I had to create space for them.

"My mother thinks I am too aggressive, but I have to be, otherwise I am treated like a child. For example, some people don't speak to me directly, but ask my mother what is wrong with me. I refuse to allow this.

"The hardest struggle was coming to terms with myself as a woman. I didn't know how to see myself. Was I a woman or was I a girl? I had to think what a woman is. Women are often presented as sexy in magazines and on television. Their ability to have babies is also stressed. I had to struggle to find out where I fit in.

"I wondered if I would have a boyfriend. I came to the conclusion you can't depend on what other people expect of you. I had to establish my own identity and my own sexuality.

"After I sorted this out for myself I felt more confident about talking about it with other disabled people and also with men who are not disabled. This is important because men often see me as asexual – as if I am not really a woman. They don't see me as a partner in bed. They want to know if I can have sex and whether I can have children. And it's not just men, but their families as well. They want to know if I can cook and clean.

"Well, I am not going to be subjected to this! I'm going to call the shots. I can see my own womanhood clearly. I am going to fall in love and out of love like anyone else. I won't allow anyone to think of me as less than a woman!"

SPEAK 56, 1993
Bitter-sweet memories by Nomboniso Gaza

On Friday 1 October 1993, Thenjiwe Mtintso broke the rules of African tradition. She chose to use the memorial service of her lover and comrade Skenjana Roji to defend the choice they made years ago to live together.

The South African Communist Party and the African National Congress "forgot" to mention her in a pamphlet which paid tribute to Skenjana.

The pamphlet about his life read: "He is survived by his mother, father, six sisters and one brother." No mention is made of Thenjiwe, with whom he chose to live for many years.

We, the women who attended the service, were ashamed of our organisations. When Thenjiwe walked into the hall where the service was being held we wanted to protect her. We did not want her to see the pamphlet. But how could she not look at the programme for the memorial service of her lover?

She read the pamphlet and decided to stand up and talk about her relationship with Skenjana. Thenjiwe openly and clearly challenged our society, the SACP, ANC and COSATU. Why had they ignored her partnership with Skenjana? She told the crowd that people must learn to accept that not everyone agrees with the rules set by society.

Many people will say Thenjiwe should have been more careful about what she said. However, with courage and strength she spoke about how she felt. She said it was her right to be recognised as the woman who was in a partnership with this man.

Had she been silent, it would have been a betrayal of Skenjana and the choice they had made together.

As a soldier she turned that hall into a battlefield. As a political educator she educated us. We listened with bitter-sweet feelings.

We were sad that she had to fight this battle on that sad day. We were proud and even happy that she had taken it up. We admired her courage. We nodded our heads to show that we agreed with her. We looked at her with pride, sadness and joy. Go on, sister. Go on! Kubo!

As she spoke, our eyes comforted her. With our hearts, we touched her. With our tears we helped her to cry. Because we were the women she was talking to.

When Thenjiwe said, "the personal is political", many of us felt a bit guilty. This was something we often forget. She said the struggles we are fighting in our personal lives are important. For the sake of peace in the home, many strong women choose to wash the dishes and ignore the oppression they face in their homes. But, in fact, it is this struggle which is central to our daily lives and struggle as feminists.

Thenjiwe spoke of the need to practice what we preach in our personal lives. At the end of it all, we were left with ourselves and our thoughts. There is a need to balance the political and the personal aspects of our lives, to love and be loved, to appreciate and be appreciated.

She showed a lot of courage when she spoke openly and honestly about Skenjana's shyness. Many of us hide the emotional side of our being. Dealing with the regime and exile meant that we had to be strong, and not show any signs of weakness.

Our society also decides that men should be strong and not have or show emotions. Women are expected to be soft, gentle and tender. Sometimes women in the struggle for equality have been expected to be as strong as men in order to be accepted. The time has come for all of us, women and men to drop our shields. To be human again – to accept ourselves. To cry, laugh, love and enjoy life. Perhaps we will find that being honest and open with those closest to us will make us more useful and strong in our struggle. Maybe the most powerful struggle is the one that is inside all of us.

Thenjiwe said what she believed needed to be said in the most difficult situation. This is our tribute to you, sister. Thank you for doing it for us, the women and men in the hall. In doing it for yourself you have done it for all of us, with courage, and strength, and beauty. So much beauty. You did it.

SPEAK 60, 1994

The pain of polygamy

Setsabile squats sadly next to an open fire as she absent-mindedly pokes a stick into the ground, thinking of where her children's next meal will come from. Her five-year-old son, Vezamafa, walks cautiously towards her, his deep set eyes hopeful, yet expecting the worst. "Is there any food, mama?" he asks. Setsabile says the words she is beginning to hate: "No, my son."

Her husband Mcondo lives with another wife and family, a few kilometres away from Setsabile and her three children.

"I will never forget the day he told me he was going to marry that woman. I am a

111

second wife and I knew that sooner or later my husband would take another wife. He used to come home three times a week, spending the other time with his first wife. He cared for the kids and made sure they were well-fed. But now he has taken a third wife. We do not see him for months."

Setsabile was six months pregnant when her husband married. According to custom, Mcondo is supposed to treat his three wives and families fairly and equally and provide for them all. But like many other men he does not do this.

"What is most painful," says Setsabile, "is that I have to beg for food for my children while their father is alive and working."

SPEAK 65, 1994
No woman's land *by Rosalee Telela*

Antoinette Letsheleha is like most young college students, discussing assignments or the latest music hits. However, unlike other students she cannot talk about where she goes to "jol" or who her real friends are.

Letsheleha (23) cannot share the joys and sorrows of her life as a black lesbian. "There are many black lesbians, but we are afraid of 'coming out of the closet' because of people's attitudes," Letsheleha told SPEAK.

When she is among her friends, at a party or club, Letsheleha publicly declares her love for other women. "I'm a lesbian. I'm attracted to other women physically, mentally and emotionally. It took me a long time to realise I was a lesbian. Although I found women attractive I had relationships with men. Then I became sexually involved with both men and women."

Letsheleha strongly believes homosexuality is neither abnormal nor un-African. "People think we have been bewitched or that we have both male and female organs. This is not true. I was not influenced by anyone. I am a lesbian woman, not a S'tabane."

Lesbian and gay pride marches and campaigns are one way in which homosexuals have made their voices heard. These marches, held in October, are becoming a tradition in South Africa.

There is, however, a price to pay when one is openly lesbian or gay.

Letsheleha says some people have become more homophobic (anti-lesbian and anti-gay). "They think lesbians are women who want to be men. But I'm not trying to be a man."

The battle for acceptance within society, and more importantly, within one's family is a difficult one. "One day a man approached me telling me how much he liked me and that we should go out together. I told him I was a lesbian. He got very angry and swore he and his friends were going to rape all lesbians to make us 'real women'. He said we were stealing their girlfriends," Letsheleha laughs nervously.

What hurts most is when your own family does not understand, she says. "It's terrible, especially if you are close to them. My sister, who is also a lesbian, and I are lucky because both our mother and grandmother have accepted us."

Although lesbian and gays still try to be accepted by their communities, they feel more at home in the company of other homosexuals. "We have our own groups where we can be comfortable with each other. We can be ourselves without any fear of being insulted and harassed," says Letsheleha.

Lesbians also experience problems similar to those of people in heterosexual relationships between a woman and a man. There is joy, love, harassment, abuse and broken relationships. "You get lesbians who abuse other women and sleep around. Some do it because they want to be like men." Letsheleha blames society for this. "They think if they act in that way society will accept them."

Megan Pillay, a member of the Gay and Lesbian Organisation of the Witwatersrand (GLOW) and the Lesbian Forum, says organising is the key to liberation for gays and lesbians. "Our organisations are there to lobby for gay and lesbian rights. Even though South Africa has a Bill of Rights which protects us, this does not mean our struggle is over."

The Bill of Rights lays down the human and civil rights of every individual. It rules out any form of discrimination on the grounds of race, gender, ethnic or social origin, colour, sexual orientation, age, disability, religion, conscience, belief, culture or language. "This has to be guarded," says Pillay. "We have to make sure that our rights are not taken away and we also still need to change people's attitudes."

Violence against gay and lesbian people is one of the most serious problems. Pillay says GLOW is working with the police to address this problem. Often the police have been accused of harassing gays and lesbians.

Letting the world know one is gay or lesbian, and even admitting it to oneself, is not easy. People often need support. There are organisations which provide counselling and support for gay and lesbian people.

Sexism within gay and lesbian organisations is a another big problem. "Whether we like it or not, we live in a sexist society. Within our organisations, it is gay men who dominate," says Pillay.

She says the Lesbian Forum, which was part of GLOW, broke away because of this. Some members of the Lesbian Forum remain members of GLOW. "A lot of lesbians feel more comfortable among each other. We meet to share similar experiences and problems."

Pillay has dreams of developing this further. "I think we should start doing things we've talked about – writing our stories, making films, looking at lesbian women's health issues. We must make sure our rights as women and lesbians are protected.

A Woman's Right to Choose

In the 1990s SPEAK reported on the abortion laws and stimulated discussion on the issue of abortion.

SPEAK 31, 1990
THE SILENCE MUST STOP! – Talking about abortion

Abortion is a very difficult thing to talk about. Most religions believe abortion is a sin. The law in South Africa at present allows abortion only under certain circumstances. Most women do not qualify for these legal abortions. This forces around 300 000 women to risk their lives every year in back-street abortions in South Africa. Because of the harmful and unclean methods many thousands of women die from unsafe abortions. Many more are emotionally and physically scarred for life.

At present only four out of every ten women who apply for a legal abortion get one. Most of these are white women. At the present time the Department of National Health and Population Development is rethinking the abortion laws and have asked people to write to them with their views.

Lerato told us about her neighbour in Soweto who died from a back-street abortion. "She was in her early thirties, and had four children. Her eldest was twelve, her youngest was one year and six months old. Her story is a very sad one. She had just got a job after staying at home for a long time. Then she fell pregnant. The family needed her job, so my neighbour, her husband and mother in law agreed she must have the abortion. There was no way the family could look after another child. I don't know where she went to get the abortion. But it didn't work." Lerato's neighbour became very sick as a result and eventually died.

The law stops women from safe abortions but it cannot stop women from risking their lives by finding other ways to end unwanted pregnancies. There are many reasons why women decide not to continue a pregnancy. As in Lerato's neighbour's

Graphic: Karen Hurt

case, the family may not be able to cope with another child. A woman might be worried about losing her job. Sometimes schoolgirls fall pregnant and are faced with the choice of having a baby or finishing their studies.

Is it right that these women are forced to find back-street abortions which are often a death sentence?

Temba, a trade-union organiser who lives in Alexandra township near Johannesburg, said, "Back-street abortions are very, very dangerous. As a Catholic I believe that as soon as the foetus has been conceived, there is life in it and it is murder to get rid of it. But one should look at abortion as one who lives in this society. I live in Alexandra township and there are many abortions there. Many women die. I was woken by a neighbour one night to take somebody to hospital. She died."

For a long time very few organisations in South Africa even mentioned abortion. Like many other things in women's lives, this was hidden. But this is changing. In 1987 women at a COSATU education conference discussed abortion as one of the issues affecting women. They were concerned about the deaths resulting from back-street abortions and asked COSATU to take up the fight for safe, free and legal abortions.

In 1990 a conference of South Africa health organisations, students, women and ANC representatives in Maputo agreed that women should be able to choose an abortion and that safe abortions should be provided with back-up counselling services.

SPEAK 51, 1993
A woman's choice

In the eyes of the law, Thandi is a criminal. She had an illegal abortion in one of the back-street abortion "clinics" in Soweto. She was eighteen and in matric when she fell pregnant. "I had no desire to have a baby, because I wanted to complete school. My parents would not understand and my boyfriend wanted nothing to do with the baby. I knew I could not care for a baby the way it should be cared for."

Today Thandi is 25 and happily married with two children. "I had my children at a time when I was able to raise them. I had a good job, I was married and could give them a home and education." Thandi does not regret her decision to have the abortion.

Abortion is a matter of life and death for thousands of South Africa women each year. The Abortion Reform Action Group (ARAG) believes women should have complete control over their own bodies. "Abortion should be legal, free and available, at least in the first three months of pregnancy," says Chris Diamond, ARAG spokesperson in Johannesburg.

Glynis Newbury of the Pro-Life organisation says, "Abortion under any circumstances is murder." But the large numbers of women who have illegal abortions every year show women "voting with their feet" in favour of access to abortion.

Graphic: Shamim

116

WOMEN AND FEAR – Paulinah Phungwayo, literacy learner

Women have more fear that men.
Some do not talk about it.
They fear the men will say they are useless.
Some who want to go to learn fear to go out.
They fear their men because the men do not
want them to go out.
    Men want to be in control.
Women have fear when they do not have beauty
or dress nice.
They fear the man will go for other women.
For the whole life the woman spends time to
make herself beautiful.
    Our men must take us the way we are.
They must stop making us into toys,
things they can pick up and throw down.
We are tired of this.
    I want to support all women. To stop having
fear.
I have seen many women who did not get the
education.
I want to say to all women:
do not be stopped by your husband to learn.
We must all learn to break this fear and the
silence.

A LADY OF LEISURE – Ayesha Badat

Here is a poem I have written. I am a mother of five and a grandmother of two. I am a saleswoman and run a small shop in Maritzburg. My formal education ended when I finished standard four as my parents didn't think that a girl should be educated.

I've washed the dishes, scrubbed the floors,
Polished the lounge, dusted the doors,
The washing is hanging out on the line,
I only hope the weather stays fine.
The ironing for once, is up to date
(Though that's the job I most hate).
I've done the shopping, baked some cakes.
I've worked so hard, how my head aches.

I've weeded the garden, cut the grass,
Shampooed the carpet, cleaned the brass.
I've defrosted the fridge, mended a fuse,
Hurried and scurried, with no time to lose.

I've sewn the button back on a shirt,
Put up the hem of my daughter's new skirt.
Windows are cleaned, the salad is made,
Supper is cooked, the table is laid.

Hubby walks in and what does he say?
Not darned that sock?
But you've had all day.

CHAPTER FIVE

Women in Political Resistance

Almost every political organisation resisting apartheid had a women's wing – a women's organisation which was separate but at the same time a part of the organisation. During the 1980s and 1990s these organisations took up bread-and-butter issues, linking them to the national liberation struggle. And at times they campaigned for women's liberation both within political organisations and in the country as a whole. It was more often than not a struggle for women to get their political organisations to take women's liberation seriously. As Raymond Suttner of the ANC points out in this chapter, in male-dominated organisations such as the ANC non-sexism as a principle is given lip-service with little understanding of what this means in people's personal lives.

While women made important gains within their political organisations, the difficulties they faced points to the importance of an autonomous women's organisation, led by women and free of male control, as a vehicle for advancing women's liberation. This chapter reflects the thinking and action within some of the political organisations. It also honours the contribution made by women who gave their lives in the struggle.

Within the United Democratic Front in the 1980s there were organisations such as the Natal Organisation of Women (NOW), the United Women's Congress (UWCO) and the Federation of Transvaal Women (FEDTRAW). Each of these bodies operated independently of one another in different parts of the country. For a time they came together nationally in the UDF Women's Congress.

These organisations spoke out about the need to organise women around issues such as the high cost of living, poor housing, pass laws, the lack of maternity benefits and child care. At the same time they talked of working towards the removal of all laws and customs that acted against women.

Women from the UDF-aligned organisations in South Africa met with ANC women, who were then still in exile, at the Malibongwe Conference in the Netherlands in 1990, discussing ways of making women's freedom a part of the struggle for national liberation. This conference called for sharing housework and child care between men and women, for opposition to certain cultural and traditional practices, for changes to laws and attitudes to protect women's rights, and for the ANC and the Mass Democratic Movement to fight sexism as seriously as they fought racism.

With the unbanning of the ANC, the ANC Women's League (ANCWL) was relaunched inside South Africa. The UDF women's organisations disbanded so that their members could join and build the Women's League. While this act strengthened the Women's League, at the same time it demobilised and weakened groups that had built grassroots support and carried out practical projects for many years. This was especially so because the negotiations brought a shift from the local to the national.

At a national level the Women's League made a significant contribution. Issues targeted at its launch included plans for making sure women's needs were included in the country's constitution and the drawing up of a charter of women's rights. Within the ANC the Women's League campaigned for greater numbers of women within the national leadership. The Women's League brought a resolution to the 1991 ANC conference that at least one third of the ANC executive members must be women. Men at the conference fought this resolution. They argued that women were not ready to lead, that there were not large enough numbers of women of leadership quality and that women had to prove themselves. Women in the Women's League felt that the NEC had abandoned them. They were determined to work towards winning this demand and did so in the run-up to the 1994 elections.

The Azanian People's Organisation (AZAPO), the Workers' Organisation for Socialist Action (WOSA) and the Pan African Congress (PAC) women's organisations organised around various issues. Women in AZAPO organised self-help projects, health projects and a bursary scheme. Women in WOSA worked to combine socialism with feminism. Women in the PAC fought alongside men while simultaneously fighting "male domination and male chauvinism in a feminist cause".

In the 1970s and 1980s women within political organisations seldom called themselves feminists. But by 1992 women in these organisations and within the South African Communist Party were adopting this title. Thenjiwe Mtintso of the SACP, for example, said in 1992 that a "lively debate is needed for the development of a strong feminist movement in the country" in order to fight gender oppression which is "as criminal an offence as racial oppression, if not worse, because it creeps into our homes".

Many women suffered detentions, bannings and house arrests during the years of struggle against apartheid. Three articles in this chapter remember some of our women heroes. We remember Victoria Mxenge, an activist lawyer, executive member of NOW and treasurer of the UDF and the Release Mandela Committee, who was assassinated in 1995. We remember Ntsiki Cotoza, a young MK cadre killed in an ambush ordered by the notorious CCB on the Swaziland border in 1988.

In the third article, women speak out about their experiences in detention: the verbal abuse, the fear of rape that is always present when they are in jail, and the knowledge that their young children feel they have deserted them.

Women in South Africa today are ensuring that women's experiences at the hands of the apartheid regime are not ignored. The Truth and Reconciliation Commission held a series of hearings for women after it was brought to its attention that women's experiences were not coming through in the general hearings. Opening the women's hearings in Johannesburg in August 1997, Thenjiwe Mtintso, then head of the Commission for Gender Equality, said: "Crimes against women are very specific and different from those experienced by men. Men did not have to endure the constant threat of rape by their captors or comments like 'You've joined these men because you've failed as a woman. You are with these men because you are an unpaid prostitute.'"

A member of the ANC Youth League told these hearings how she was repeatedly raped by four men who continually shouted abuse. Later she was taken to a doctor who was told she was a prostitute picked up in Hillbrow. Until her testimony before the Truth Commission she had never told her mother the truth about what had happened to her in detention. "I was ashamed. I thought I'd done something to deserve to be treated like this." Many women expressed this feeling of shame. Evidence was given of women prisoners forced to do star-jumps naked, of rats and other objects being inserted into women's vaginas, of women being told their children were ill or dead.

The following articles focus on women in political organisations during the years of struggles against apartheid. The next chapter highlights the political activism of women during the years of negotiations.

FROM THE PAGES OF *SPEAK*

SPEAK 4, 1984
National Women's Day

Wathint' abafazi,
wathint' imbokotho.
You have tampered with the women,
You have struck against a rock.

So sang more than 20 000 women outside the Union Buildings in Pretoria on 9 August 1956. The women came from all over South Africa. Some on foot, some by bus, train or car. Some had babies on their backs. They had travelled long distances to protest against the pass laws for women. For 30 minutes the women stood in silence. Four of them went into the building to hand in a petition demanding an end to the pass laws.

This day of unity and strength among women is remembered every 9 August by women in all parts of South Africa.

Natal Organisation of Women

The Natal Organisation of Women (NOW) was formed in December 1983 and launched on 9 August 1984. "The women who formed NOW had come together previously to organise National Women's Day. We felt the need to unite against problems like the high cost of living, poor housing, pass laws, the lack of proper maternity benefits, child care and many other issues. So we formed the Natal Organisation of Women.

"NOW aims to work towards the removal of all laws and customs that act against women. Immediately NOW aims to organise women around issues that affect their daily lives. We also see it as important that women take an active part in trade unions and community organisations. We have started branches and working groups in various areas."

UDF Women's Congress is launched

Women from organisations in the UDF met in Cape Town to launch a new organisation for women – the UDF Women's Congress.

The Women's Congress upholds the Freedom Charter and the Women's Charter. These two charters were drawn up in the 1950s and speak of the changes people want in South Africa. The UDF Women's Congress plans to:
- teach men and women in the UDF about women's oppression
- increase women's skills and confidence in their organisation
- do away with all forms of discrimination based on sex
- talk about women's problems in all UDF meetings and organisations.

A woman's place is in her organisation

The United Women's Congress held a conference to build the Federation of South African Women in August 1989. The theme of the conference was "Women Unite for a Future South Africa". The aim was to reach out to women across class and racial barriers. "We all want peace in our land. We are all concerned about the future of our children. We all share common experiences. Let us talk of these things. Let us talk of our problems and work out solutions. Let us talk of freedom." And the women came. Three hundred delegates from 45 organisations attended the conference. These included women from youth, civic, religious, health and service organisations. There were rural and urban women. Topics workshopped included work and unemployment, housing, health, education, children and the family, law, violence against women, culture and media, repression and religion. Women drew up demands and spoke of how they will fight for these demands.

FEDSAW Cultural Festival highlighted women's concerns – May 1989.   *Photo: Eric Miller*

SPEAK 27, 1990

MALIBONGWE CONFERENCE – South African women unite for a non-sexist post-apartheid South Africa

For the first time women from within South Africa met with women from the ANC outside the country at the Malibongwe Conference in Holland in July 1990. As one South African delegate said, "Malibongwe brought us together with our comrades in exile. Together we were able to say what we want as women, and we are prepared to work very hard to achieve what we want."

The conference was organised by the ANC Women's Section, women from South Africa and the Women's Committee of the Dutch Anti-Apartheid Movement. The aim of the conference was to make sure women's issues are taken seriously and women's freedom is a part of the struggle for national liberation.

Delegates called for housework and child care to be shared by men and women in the home. They said only when men take equal responsibility in the home will women be able to take part fully in organisations.

The conference spoke of the problems

The Malibongwe Conference held in Holland in July 1990 brought together women from exile and from inside South Africa.   *Photo: SPEAK*

123

of rural women and said there should be links between urban and rural women. The conference set up a bursary fund to develop rural women's skills. Women agreed that cultural and traditional practices that oppress women must be fought.

All agreed that women cannot be free while all people are oppressed because of race, poverty or a lack of political power. But the freedom of women won't just happen with national liberation. South Africa needs laws to protect women's rights. But this is not enough. Attitudes must change and the ANC and Mass Democratic Movement must fight sexism as seriously as they fight racism.

SPEAK 27, 1990
ANC and SACP unbanned

People are singing and toyi-toying all over South Africa. The organisations of the people have been unbanned. Comrade Nelson Mandela is out of prison!

SPEAK 28, 1990
Women's liberation must be part of new South Africa

A number of meetings in March 1990 focused on women in the new South Africa.

At an International Women's Day meeting in Johannesburg Helen Joseph said, "It is your job as women to see that women are going to be recognised in the new South Africa."

Judith Howadeen of the Black Sash said, "As women of South Africa we can be proud of our tradition of resistance, but the time has come to look forward. We must make sure our voices are heard in the new constitution. We must end the present situation where it is men who make the laws. We must challenge the ANC to include women to play a pivotal role."

Sister Bernard said, "Women must be present at the negotiating table. The ANC must be asked what is happening to a non-sexist South Africa. It is not the men who are going to make it happen for us. It is us who are going to make it happen, not only for us, but also for them. Plunge, swim and get to that liberated South Africa."

At a national UDF and COSATU Women's Workshop in March, Firoza Adam of the Federation of Transvaal Women said, "It is important for us to unite women committed to a non-racial, non-sexist, democratic South Africa. Otherwise we will find ourselves in the same situation as women in other countries in the post-liberation era. After having struggled together with their men for liberation, women comrades found their position had not changed. We need to assert our position as women more strongly now than ever before and we can only do that effectively as one, unified, loud voice."

SPEAK 31, 1990
South African Communist Party launched

On 29 July 1990 the SACP was launched after many years in exile and operating underground. Geraldine Fraser Moleketi and Essop Pahad told SPEAK of the SACP view on women's oppression. "The SACP is very aware that black women suffer triple oppression - as blacks, as women and as workers. We have recognised for some time that there can be no real liberation without the liberation of women. But to act on this may take longer than we would like it to. The SACP believes that there must be action to make sure that women play a leading role in all party structures. We want to get more women into the party as members."

SPEAK 33, 1991
A LONG AND DIFFICULT ROAD – Building the ANC Women's League

The ANC Women's League was launched in August 1990. By January 1991 there were 655 branches of the ANC and 450 branches of the Women's League. We spoke to Khosi Xaba, an organiser for the ANC Women's League.

She told us, "We see three main issues we need to look at. The constitution and the discussion around this, the Charter of Women's Rights and the literacy campaign. We would like projects to be educative and income-generating so that branches can support themselves."

The Women's League has set up a task force of 21 members and three organisers to build the League. One problem that has caused some tension among women is that most of the women on the task force are returned exiles. Khosi said, "It is a bit of a problem. People are saying the League is from outside, that we are bound to make mistakes and we are out of touch with the situation. It is a problem we cannot solve as people from the outside. The task force says that to resolve this people must build branches and regional structures and have elections."

SPEAK 36, 1991
We've got the future looking at us

The ANC Women's League tried to introduce an affirmative action policy at the July 1991 conference. They failed – but the debate will never be the same again.

July 1991 was hot in Durban. Sizzling hot. It wasn't even summer. In fact it wasn't the weather at all – it was the heated debate around the ANC Women's League proposal on women and leadership. The proposal was that the ANC constitution should put affirmative action into practice by saying that at least 30% of the positions on the National Executive (NEC) be filled by women.

Anyone who can do a bit of arithmetic would say that 30% sounds like little – seeing that women make up 52% of South Africa's population. But up until this point no women have been elected among the six national ANC office-bearers. And there are only nine women out of the 50 other elected members of the ANC NEC. This gives only 18% of the NEC seats to women. The Women's League was proposing that women make up one third of the NEC.

Not everybody agreed with this strategy of affirmative action. Even some individuals in the Women's League were against it. They say that just because a woman is voted into power, this doesn't mean that she is going to fight women's oppression and exploitation. Britain's Maggie Thatcher was a good example of this!

Perhaps the most important thing about the 30% proposal at the conference was the debate it produced. We saw many fine examples of sexist attitudes within the liberation movement. And it showed that women have to prepare, educate and organise at a grassroots level to pull off this kind of proposal. It also proved that even when you are promised support from senior leadership, it doesn't mean that you will get it.

Delegates who stood up to speak said some interesting things. One respected male delegate said that having a 30% clause in the constitution would set a precedent for "minority rights". (Women were shocked – 52% of the population cannot count as a minority in any language.) Some said that the 30% clause should be in ANC policy, not in the constitution. Others argued that women are "not ready to lead", that there aren't enough women of "leadership quality", that women must "prove themselves".

Some of these arguments should sound familiar to black people in this country. After all – these are the arguments that whites have used to hold onto power all these years!

Joe Slovo, who was chairing the session, wanted to put the proposal to the vote – but the Women's League blocked this by announcing that they would not take part. So the vote was stopped.

Baleka Kgotsisile, secretary general of the Women's League, explains the reasons for stopping the vote. She says that the women saw their proposal as putting affirmative action into practice. The December 1990 ANC consultative conference had already committed itself to affirmative action and therefore they believed that this was not an issue to be voted on.

Another important reason for stopping the vote was that the Women's League felt that if the vote was lost, it would be like losing the vote for affirmative action.

Baleka says that it was obvious that the women did not want just any women in leadership positions. They wanted delegates to look particularly at women with leadership skills. She says, "Affirmative action does not mean tokenism. Affirmative action goes along with quality.

"I am disappointed in the old NEC leadership. They could have made their positions clear without forcing delegates to agree. The women were clearly very angry – they felt the NEC had abandoned them."

Baleka believes that affirmative action for women and for black people in this country is a way of trying to do something about the inequalities of the past. "For people who have been historically pushed down, there is a need to work out ways of

SPEAK

1990   R1.00   No. 30

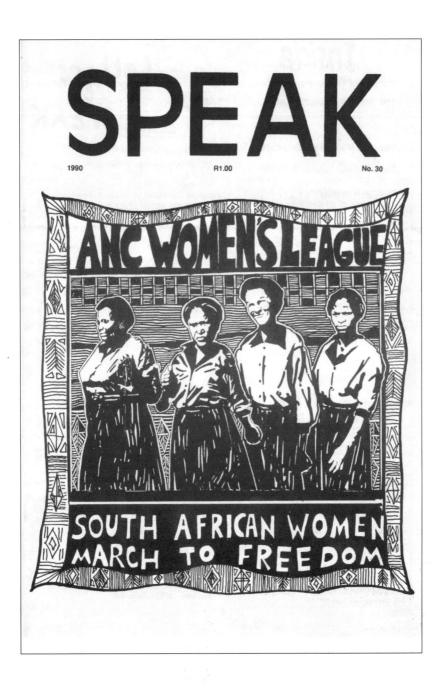

ANC WOMEN'S LEAGUE

SOUTH AFRICAN WOMEN MARCH TO FREEDOM

reversing the effects of oppression. For example, we must address the fact that women are under-represented in most areas of life except traditional women's roles."

Baleka attributes the failure of the 30% strategy to the fact that the Women's League had not done enough work in regional and branch structures. Other critics have said that the Women's League could have given more guidance. They failed to come up with alternative strategies when it was clear that the 30% proposal would not win.

Baleka feels that they learned a lot from what happened at the conference. She says that the way forward is to increase the debate within the ANC. The Women's League wants the ANC to set up a national commission on the emancipation of women. She says there's lots of work ahead.

The biggest question this debate at conference raised seems to be: how can the words "affirmative action" be put into real practice? And how can women ensure that this issue is placed very high on the agenda of a male-dominated liberation movement along with non-racialism and democracy?

"We've got the future looking at us," says Baleka. "We must plan workshops and we must put pressure on the national leadership to make sure that the new constitution ensures the emancipation of women. This is where the ANC Women's League campaign for a charter for women's rights comes in."

SPEAK 36, 1991
AZAPO and women

Rose Ngwenya, the president of Imbeleko, AZAPO's women's wing said,"AZAPO promotes socialism. We have workers' interests at heart and believe in starting at the grassroots. What we want to see is all people treated as equals, and this can only happen under socialism. For capitalism to survive, somebody down there is exploited, and we know blacks are being exploited for the well-being of the rich.

"We have Imbeleko because we know that women have unique problems. Imbeleko concentrates on women's affairs. We encourage women to be self-reliant, not to depend on men. Imbeleko runs self-help projects. We provide training in bricklaying, carpentry, and upholstery. We run a health project. Another project is the Adopt to Educate project. Bursaries are given to high-school and college students."

SPEAK 37, 1991
WOSA on women

Kate Truscott of WOSA told us: "We think WOSA is the only independent socialist organisation in South Africa. We see ourselves as part of the broad liberation movement, but because we are a socialist organisation we can put forward the interests and position of the working class without compromising them. We see the national liberation movement as vague on worker issues. WOSA is an anti-capitalist, pro-working class, socialist organisation."

On WOSA's position on women Kate said, "The women's commission is still being consolidated. We try to formulate a political position on women's oppression in South Africa and we try to work with other women in a united-front way. It is only recently that there is space for something called socialist feminism. It is very important to combine feminism and socialism.

"My own view is that we need an independent women's movement in this country. We think women's demands can best be taken up in a mass-based women's movement. This will be more effective than each women's organisation within other structures making demands. Women's oppression is so overwhelming. A women's movement can offer a support system, solidarity and sisterhood to encourage women to identify issues and move into struggle to take these up."

SPEAK 38, 1992

The PAC and women *by Shamim Meer*

Ellen Mothopeng, publicity secretary of the PAC's African Women's Organisation (AWO) told us, "We aim to rally African women under the banner of African nationalism and to educate women socially, politically, morally and to conscientise them.

"AWO was launched in Katlehong on 6 April 1986. We have had many programmes such as calls for the release of the Sharpville Six. We focused on Theresa Ramashamola and campaigned for her release.

"AWO sees national oppression and sexual oppression as two sides of the same coin. We are committed to fighting colonial oppression alongside our male comrades as well as fighting against male domination and male chauvinism as sisters in the feminist cause.

"AWO will campaign to ensure women make up no less than half of the PAC leadership. We have dealt with things like sexual harassment. We need to educate women about the Constituent Assembly, about elections. We need to draw up constitutional clauses which protect women and children from the injustices they face."

SPEAK 41, 1992

Yes, I am a feminist! *by Glenda Daniels*

In the past, feminism was a dirty word in many political organisations and black progressive circles. Many people thought feminism was only for white, middle-class women. They said feminism divided the people, and black women should concentrate on fighting apartheid and not fight men. But today many women are not afraid to say they are feminists.

Baleka Kgotsisile, general secretary of the ANC Women's League says, "I am a feminist who works full-time for a women's organisation. We focus on issues which are central not only to middle-class women but to all women, especially the historically disadvantaged African women. They continue to be abused, raped, battered and so on. How then can people argue that we should not have feminism?" Kgositsile said people should be focusing on feminism in South Africa "because this is a time to bring about a better future for all our people, including women, who have always been at the bottom of the pile".

Ellen Mothopeng, president of the PAC African Women Organisation, said feminism does exist in South Africa but not to the same degree as in countries overseas. She said she did not want to call herself a feminist but that at times women are forced to be feminists because of the way men behave. "When we challenge men in the PAC, they say the organisation has only Africanists, not men and women. They don't want to recognise the difference." Mothopeng said there was need for feminism in South Africa because all women are sisters, regardless of political beliefs. She said women are fighting for recognition in politics and for power to oppose oppressive customary laws. "It is important to educate men about feminism too, so they don't label you a dangerous woman."

Thenjiwe Mtintso of the SACP said, "A strong feminist movement is needed to change the unequal, unfair relations between men and women in society." Mtintso said working-class women also have feminist views. "In the labour movement, working-class women raise feminist concerns like equal pay for equal work, maternity and paternity leave, child care facilities at work and the fight against violence against women at work."

Mtintso said lively debate is needed for the development of a strong feminist movement in the country. For example, we need to talk about whether it is possible for women of different races and classes to unite together as sisters.

Unfortunately, she added, time is running out for this kind of debate as change is taking place quickly and women have to get involved in that process. "For instance, as it stands now, CODESA is almost completely a man's world, dotted with a few women. We argue that gender oppression is as criminal an offence as racial oppression, if not worse, because it creeps into the privacy of our homes. Therefore it must be part of the discussion on the future of South Africa."

Mtintso said there was a time in the liberation struggle when it was felt all energy had to be united to "fight the common enemy". "This is now outdated. There was also the wrong belief that national liberation will automatically mean the liberation of women."

Kate Truscott, national co-ordinator of the Women's Commission of WOSA, said there was a need for an independent organisation. "There is a growing feminist awareness in unions, rape crisis centres, in the townships around health issues and child care, and in the student movement around sexual harassment. Sexual harassment needs to be addressed urgently as well as women's health because of the high level of cervical cancer in the country."

"Yes, I am a feminist," said Rose Ngwenya, president of Imbeleko, the AZAPO women's organisation. "There is a whole generation of women who won't admit to

SPEAK

1990   R1.00   No. 27

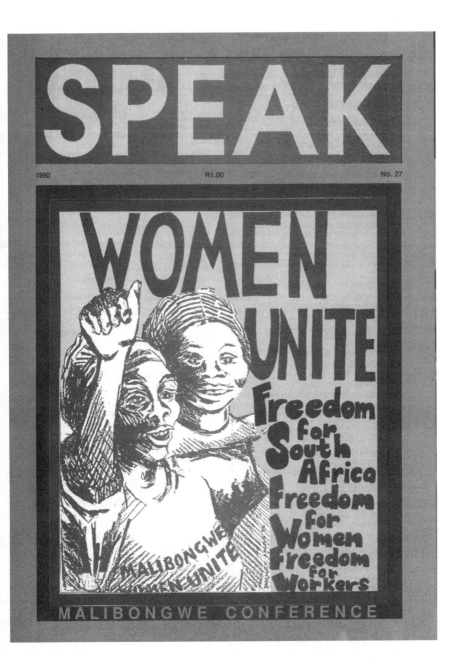

being feminists because of the propaganda spread by the media, which is controlled by men and gives a false picture of feminism as middle-class and Western."

Ngwenya believes working-class women do believe in feminism. She said AZAPO is educating its members about non-sexism. "This does not mean sexism does not exist in the organisation. The need for feminist awareness will always exist. The oppression of women is an international problem and is as old and common as dirt itself."

SPEAK 56, 1993
Inside the ANC

In 1993 Immanuel Suttner (no relation) interviewed ANC Political Education head and NEC member Raymond Suttner on sexism in the ANC.

SPEAK: The ANC has called for a non-racial and non-sexist South Africa. Do ANC leaders and grassroots supporters practise non-sexism?

SUTTNER: The acceptance of non-sexism as a principle in the ANC, or any male-dominated organisation, appears in the first place at the level of lip-service. There is a strong commitment to the principle of non-sexism. But for people to realise its full significance is still in the beginning stages. And I am not sure there is a real and full understanding of what it means for people in their personal lives. My experience in the democratic movement is that there a quite a lot of abuse of women. I remember, in the days before the unbannings, cases of women being beaten up by men and even rapes. So I think there is a lot of work to do to make non-sexism a reality.

SPEAK: How can we make non-sexism a reality?

SUTTNER: We have something very strong (and it's a terrible, terrible way to talk about it) that we can build on, and that is the memory of Chris Hani. Chris Hani was very committed to non-sexism. In MK, he worked hard to get rid of sexist practices: women washing uniforms of commanders, officers having relationships with women trainees. In the SACP, he made sure that there was a gender desk, and he himself was involved in that. So one of the things we should do when we honour Chris Hani is not to remember him as some charismatic figure, but as someone we can learn from.

SPEAK: How practically can we overcome the problem of male domination in the ANC and begin to empower women?

SUTTNER: In terms of empowering women, it is a long road. It's one thing to say men and women must be treated as equals. But I think, culturally, women – especially African women – have been given far fewer opportunities than men. It is now a question of creating special training opportunities which will give women a chance to develop leadership skills. To be quite frank, our department does not have the resources to do this for men, let alone women, but is one of the things that remains important for us.

SPEAK: You talk about special leadership training for women. Would this be a form of affirmative action?

SUTTNER: I do not like this term "affirmative action". It comes from the [United States of] America, where minorities were trying to get a better life in American society. In South Africa, we are talking about a complete change in our society, especially in relation to the economy. Women are not a minority, and really we need to change society as a whole.

SPEAK: How do you see South African society in the future?

SUTTNER: We will be a mainly African nation and will move away from the way that European society has been forced on people. But the new South African nation we want to build will not mean an end to the different cultures in our country. People will be able to practise their own cultures. We will not be a nation which on the day of freedom will make everyone speak Zulu. We will speak different languages. We will have different colours and we will follow different cultures. The question is how to bring everyone together in a way that we will have the non-racial, non-sexist, democratic society which the ANC speaks of.

SPEAK: What will happen in a case where a person does something that goes against the democratic principles of society, but which is accepted in that person's culture?

SUTTNER: One such example is sexism, where a lot of work needs to be done. Unfortunately we come from a history where problems are solved through violence. The ANC doesn't want to come to power and solve problems through violence and force. What is important is to change people's ideas, and that is why I would like to continue working in political education of the public at large.

Heroes of the Struggle

The following articles are about assassinations and battles that raged in various communities. Subsequent evidence, including that of the Truth and Reconciliation Commission, has pointed to police and third-force activity as directly responsible for the assassinations and the political violence. Many brave fighters of apartheid lost their lives during the years of struggle. These included community activists and MK guerrillas. We pay tribute to all the heroes and remember them all through the stories of some reflected here.

ANC members in a show of solidarity at a funeral in 1990.   *Photo: Gille, You and Me Images*

SPEAK 7, 1984

United action in the Transvaal

On 5 and 6 November, 800 000 workers and 400 000 students took part in a stay-away in the Transvaal. This was the first time that so many people in South Africa protested together. It was also the first time since the 1960s that trade unions, students, community organisations and women showed their strength together.

Since February 1994, school pupils have been on boycott because they want changes in the education system. Many schools were closed down and at least 150 people were killed and many more injured. A few weeks before the stayaway, 7 000 police and soldiers went into Sebokeng township very early one morning. They entered and searched every home in the township. They arrested many of the community representatives.

Student, worker, community and women's organisations then came together to form the Transvaal Regional Stayaway Committee. Their main demands were that the army and police move out of the townships, that rent and bus fare increases be stopped, that the age limit in schools be abolished and that elected student representative councils be recognised as the true voice of the students.

Victoria Mxenge

Victoria Mxenge was brutally murdered outside her home in Umlazi on 1 August 1985. Four men shot and axed her to death. The news of this terrible murder has horrified, shocked and saddened people, especially those who knew and worked with her. Victoria was involved in many organisations. She was an executive member of the Natal Organisation of Women, treasurer of the United Democratic Front and treasurer of the Release Mandela Committee. She was a lawyer for the treason trial in Pietermartizburg.

Victoria's husband Griffiths Mxenge was assassinated in 1981. The murderers have not yet been found. Their three children Mbasa, Viwe and Nomhle have suffered the loss of both parents in this terrible way. Both Victoria and Griffiths were involved in working for a better society. Griffiths spent some years on Robben Island.

To protest against Victoria's death the Natal Organisation of Women organised a placard demonstration on Durban's streets. The UDF and other organisations called protest meetings. A NOW speaker, Nozizwe, spoke about the loss that comes with Victoria's death and about Victoria as a woman, experiencing many of the problems of women under apartheid. She said these problems will end only by women uniting together.

Over the past months many who fought apartheid have mysteriously disappeared or died. Victoria's death follows the brutal murders of four UDF and Cradock Residents' Association leaders – Matthew Goniwe, Fort Calata, Sicelo Mhlawuli and Sparrow Mkhonto. These killings come at a time when the government has declared a state of emergency in most parts of the country.

Women on the march

It was a sight people in Johannesburg had not seen for a long time. Women were marching down the street, singing of a free South Africa. Heads came to windows of office buildings. People came out of shops. "Who are these women?" they asked. The women are making their voices heard against the bannings of organisations and the restrictions on leaders such as Albertina Sisulu. Against the repressive laws of this country and especially the Labour Relations Bill.

The day of protest took place on International Women's Day and was organised by the Federation of Transvaal Women.

A fighting life

Ntsiki Cotoza was one of several young MK cadres killed in an ambush on the Swaziland border. Many years later a policeman confessed that they were under orders from the notorious CCB to eliminate the travellers. Her mother told SPEAK the story of her life.

In a house in Lamontville a woman sits at her kitchen table. It is cool and dark outside. There is the sound of buses and taxis. People are arriving home from work. The woman has lots of silver hair. She has a strong face, but she looks tired and sad. Her name is Zizile.

Not so long ago Zizile had three daughters. Now she has only two. She show us photographs of her daughter Nontsikilelo. She is proud of Ntsiki. There is a photo of Ntsiki with her baby son Lunga. We look at the photographs; they make us feel sad. Ntsiki looks so young. We watch Lunga, Ntsiki's son. He is running in and out of the room.

Zizile Cotoza is the mother of Nontsikilelo, who was killed by the police in June 1988. She was killed together with seven other young people at the Swaziland border. Police said they killed them because they were members of the African National Congress.

SPEAK has come to talk to Zizile about her daughter's short life. Zizile wants to tell the story to the whole world. "Ntsiki was my second child. She was born in June 1967 in Lamontville Hospital. She went to school in the township here and she was a very brilliant child."

Zizile said, "When Ntsiki was doing standard eight I received a letter from her school. The teacher was complaining about Ntsiki, saying she was one of the students causing problems at school. Ntsiki said that students wanted the school to be a better place to learn. The school building was old and they wanted it repaired. There were not enough teachers. They also found it very hard to learn in the presence of the police and SADF. The army would throw teargas and would sjambok students every time they tried to get together to discuss their problems.

"Ntsiki told me no one would listen to the students' problems. Instead teachers and inspectors said the students were causing problems. During those days things were very bad at Lamontville High School. I remember one day Ntsiki and her friends were chased by police and they jumped out of the window. Ntsiki was lucky not to be injured. But one of her friends was so badly hurt she will never walk again.

"Ntsiki was doing standard nine when she fell pregnant. She continued at school until she had the baby. She loved her son very much. I had to accept the situation and let her go back to school. She used to come home in the middle of the day and breastfeed Lunga.

"Ntsiki was becoming very unhappy with her school life in South Africa. I remember her saying that she didn't want to carry on staying here. I did not take her seriously. I was sure she could not leave Lunga behind. She loved him very much. She spoke of a new South Africa that she dreamt of and she spoke of the need to fight in order to change things in the country. I feared for her life, but she taught me to be strong and brave. She said, 'Ma, whose child do you want to have die for the struggles of this country? Be brave and expect that your child will die one day.'

"Ntsiki was being harassed by police. She hid from them, taking her nine-month-old baby on her back. But they found her and both were detained for three weeks. Ntsiki tried to leave the country once, but the police caught her and she was detained again.

"When Lunga was three years old Ntsiki disappeared again. He spent four months crying for her. He would run out of the gates following anyone who looked like Ntsiki. My heart was sore. I did everything to make Lunga happy, but he was missing his mom. I knew that Ntsiki was missing him too.

"She did write to say that she was safe. She said she was at school. But most of all she wanted to know how Lunga was.

"On 8 June this year I saw that young people were killed at the Swaziland border. I felt bad about it but I never thought one of those people could be my child. I saw the kombi they were said to have been in. It looked badly damaged.

"The police came one night to show me photographs of my daughter dead. I did not cry in front of them because that is what they wanted. I was very angry at being woken up only to be shown photographs of my child dead. I was angry that they had killed her. Why was she not arrested and tried in court if she did wrong?

"I went to see the lawyers. They helped me and the other parents to find a way to see the bodies of our children." Zizile said it was a long silent journey from Durban to Piet Retief to identify her child's body. They were taken to a room where the bodies were. Zizile said, "There was a terrible smell. We saw our children piled together. Some were put on top of the others. Ntsiki's body was badly damaged and I could hardly recognise her. I was upset, but mostly I was very angry."

All Zizile told Lunga was that his mother was killed in an accident. She thought he was too young to understand. But recently Zizile got a big surprise. Lunga saw some police and he started becoming very angry. He told Zizile that he hates police because they killed his mother. He is only four, but he knows what it means to hate.

Zizile is a strong woman. She says Nontsikilelo helped her to be even stronger. She said, "I have lost my child that I loved so much. But I know that she died for all the peace-loving people of this country. I'm proud of her. To all the mothers who are losing their children every day – be strong, be ready for it. Listen to your children when they tell you about their frustrations. Support them in their struggle for justice."

A call for the release of detainees at the Bend the Bars Concert in Johannesburg in February 1988.

Photo: Eric Miller

SPEAK 24, 1989

From one small jail into a bigger jail

"I think its having an effect on me now. I feel scared of people I don't know. I also can't bear people asking me too many questions. For the first two months I was interrogated daily. When people ask me questions I feel like I am being interrogated again. I must try and overcome this feeling," said Veliswa Mhlawuli. Veliswa is one of the thousands of people who have been in detention. She is a journalist with *Grassroots*, a Cape Town community newspaper which was recently banned for three months by the government for telling the truth.

We cannot write all we have heard about experiences in detention because the government does not allow us to write about detention and interrogation.

Veliswa said, "This was the first time I was ever detained. No one can imagine what it is like. It is a nightmare. I did not think that people could be treated like that." Veliswa was in jail for six months and is being charged. She has not been told the charges and at the time of SPEAK going to print she was out on bail.

In South Africa today many people are kept in detention. This is the government's way of silencing those who want to see a better life for all South Africans. Men, women and children have been detained. Since the state of emergency (three years ago) more than 300 000 people have spent time in South Africa's jails. Some have spent days, some months, and some more than three years. Detention has broken up families and left scars that will forever remind us of the suffering endured in fighting for a free South Africa.

How do security police treat women who are detained? Women get treated as badly as men. They face isolation, torture, interrogation, and lies. But the police often use something more against women detainees. They use dirty tricks. Thandi was detained for nearly a year and then released without being charged for any crime. "They try many ways to make you feel you are here because you are irresponsible, your morals are low. They use a lot of verbal abuse, they call you bitch and all sorts of things.

"Specific kinds of torture are applied to women. The whole time you fear that you can actually be raped. One of the security policemen actually suggested the best treatment for me would be rape. They can walk right into your cell and you are in solitary confinement on your own – you are exposed to that danger. They can get away with it. It's not beyond them. You are totally at their mercy.

"They also bring in your responsibility as a mother. They say, 'What kind of mother will leave their child?' They make you feel guilty about being in jail, whereas they put you in jail. My main source of worry was my child and I felt guilty at times. Later I would be convinced that I had done nothing wrong. In fact what I was doing would eventually benefit myself, my child and humanity."

Young children cannot understand why parents have suddenly disappeared from their lives. One mother said of her son's reaction to her detention, "I felt quite strongly that he felt I had deserted him. And when he did finally visit, the visits were non-contact and I don't think he understood why I wasn't reaching out and touching him."

Security police and prison officials humiliate women detainees when they are menstruating. Thandi says, "I had to go without pads for some time because the police said my lawyer should bring me pads. But I had no contact with my lawyer. Later on I found out that they are supposed to provide these things."

TODAY – Nise Malange

Everyone who has died
Is here today
Those who died in the struggle of the people
Are here
Singing with us –
They are holding our hands,
Just that touch
Moving through all our bodies
Like a bloodstream

Biko
Is here today
Neil Agget
Who died for the liberation of workers
Is here today
Ephraim Shabalala who died
The system's victim
Is here today
Andries Raditsela
Who died for us all
Is here today,
with us
sharing
This day with us.

Those who died as oppressors are here –
They weep about their past
Their hands are swollen
They cannot hold our hands
I can feel their cold breath
Brushing my shoulders.

Our babies and children who died
Because of the system
Are here playing around
On this day
They are observing and learning
From us in their next lives.

Our brothers and sisters,
Mothers and fathers
Who died confused,
Without making up their minds
Are here today
They want to put their arms around us and sing:
"Hlanganani Basebenzi."

The oppressors, the killers,
The murderers, assassins,
The traitors, the impimpis
All those who were against our people's freedom
Are wandering among us
They are looking closely
Into our eyes
They want to speak
To us about what they have done
But there is no way for us
To be aware of their presence.
Away oppressor
Away traitor
Go away
Go away.
All those who were against peace and justice
Must go away from us today
Today!

CHAPTER SIX

Women in Negotiations, Government and Civil Society

As South Africa drew closer to the negotiations that were to lead to the 1994 elections, women's organisations such as the ANC Women's League, the Women's National Coalition and the Rural Women's Movement played an important part in raising issues of concern to women. The experience of years of organisation and mobilisation came together as women realised this was their chance to make sure the new South Africa meant freedom for women too.

Once negotiations took off in the first round of multi-party negotiations, known as CODESA, women challenged male domination in the negotiations. Women pushed for and won a Gender Advisory Committee which was set up as one of CODESA's working groups. Its role was to ensure that CODESA recommendations were "non-sexist" and to advise each of the CODESA working groups on women's problems.

Through their efforts, women in the ANC won a large number of seats for women in the new parliament. In 1991 The ANC Women's League had spearheaded a movement within the party that at least one third of its National Executive Committee should be women. Although they did not win this campaign at the time, ANC women continued this battle within the ANC and won the demand that women would comprise at least one third of the candidates on the ANC's list for parliament.

The ANC Women's League was also a key player in setting up the Women's National Coalition, whose task was to consult widely with women in the country in order to bring together their key concerns within the country's Bill of Rights. The Coalition's Women's Charter was launched in 1996.

Women's efforts won the Gender Equality Clause in the new constitution of the country, so high a proportion of women in parliament that South Africa now ranks number four in the world in this respect, with 106 of the 400 MPs being women, and the putting into place of "gender machinery" at various levels of government in order to advance gender equality.

But as MP Nozizwe Madlala, writing in the first year of the new government, says – the struggle is not yet over, since in practice the situation for women has not changed despite changes in the law.

Some see a gap because South Africa does not have an independent women's movement. Discussion in the pages of SPEAK after the accession of the new government includes the following comments by Debbie Bonnin of Agenda, the South African journal about women and gender: "Women cannot pin their hopes on what women in parliament can achieve for them." Bonnin says that a national independent women's movement "will put the interests of women first, as opposed to the interests of political parties, churches, unions or civics." Asha Moodley, also a members of Agenda's editorial collective, agrees that women "need to grab power in our hands so that we can define our own agendas and policies and not just slot into the political parties".

The Women's National Coalition (WNC) probably came closest to being a movement for women in South Africa. But some see the coalition as limited because of its domination by political parties. Issues such as abortion, for example, were never resolved within the WNC because of this. A new movement is needed, says Annemarie Nutt, a WNC national executive member, which will "need to be politically independent and to organise from bottom up". Nutt sees the WNC as resembling political parties in its top-down character.

Jessie Duarte, at the time provincial MEC for Safety and Security in Gauteng, says the WNC failed to build a national women's movement in the country, although it tried. The coalition, she believes, "raised more issues of the middle class instead of issues affecting working, unemployed and women who are not organised". However, she admits the WNC made gains. "If it was not for the coalition we would not have clauses in the constitution recognising the special problems of women." Duarte says, "we have educated men on the language of gender equality but we haven't actually educated them on the reality of gender equality." She is concerned about rape and the abuse of women by men.

These issues remain concerns for women today. More recent interviews in this chapter with women from the Gauteng Provincial Legislature, the New Women's Movement and the Women's National Coalition reflect some of the issues confronting women today.

FROM THE PAGES OF *SPEAK*

The articles that follow from the pages of SPEAK reflect some of the things women were saying and doing as the country prepared for the new government. The first section looks at the period of negotiations, and the second section at women in the first year of the new South Africa.

Women Make Their Voices Heard
in the Negotiations

SPEAK 26, 1989
BE PART OF MAKING YOUR DREAM COME TRUE – Constitutional
Guidelines for a free, democratic, non-racist South Africa

The African National Congress has come up with a document called the Constitutional Guidelines. This document sets out an idea for the ANC's plans for a future South Africa. The ANC wants people and organisations in South Africa to discuss these guidelines. In this way, people in South Africa can be part of shaping our future.

For hundreds of years the majority of people in South Africa have struggled against a government that has been only interested in the needs of a small minority – the white South Africans. Black people and workers have had to fight against oppressive laws made by this white government. As part of this fight the people of South Africa and their organisations were involved in drawing up the Freedom Charter in 1955. At this time the ANC was a legal organisation in South Africa. The ANC's Constitutional Guidelines were drawn up in 1987 by the ANC outside South Africa. The guidelines spell out more clearly how the demands of the Freedom Charter can become part of the future South Africa.

Many organisations have started to discuss the guidelines. It is important that they are discussed all over South Africa. Women and men need to say what we want to see in a new South Africa. It is now that we have a chance to play a part not only in struggling against the old system, but also in shaping the new society. As Nomvula, a woman active in the trade unions, said, "It is important to discuss these guidelines. We can be part of adding to or changing them. We can say what we want in a post-apartheid South Africa. When freedom comes we must know what we are going to do with it."

The guidelines are based on democracy and an end to racism and sexism. The document talks about creating a society in which people will be able to lead normal, decent lives, as free citizens in a free country. It talks about having a government in which people will have a say at all levels.

One section of the guidelines deals with women's rights. It says women must have the same rights as men at home, at work and in the community. That the state will give women special help to make up for the inequalities of the past. We asked women from women's organisations what they understood by this. And what they wanted to see in a future, free South Africa. "What will it mean to have the same rights as men at home, work, and in the community?" we asked.

Shehnaz said, "The ANC wants a situation where women will no longer be op-

144

ANC Women's League members discuss gender and CODESA in 1992.

Photo: Elmond Jiyane, CDC Photo Unit

pressed and exploited. Women will have to stand up for their rights and men will have to learn that they cannot have their own way. We will be able to fight things like rape, and wife-beating. As women we will have a place in the new society that we can be proud of. The struggles alongside our men against apartheid and capitalism are going to mean a real change for us as women."

Nomvula said, "Marriage must not be a burden. It must be a partnership. Bringing up children must not be the duty of women. Men must take part in everything from washing nappies to feeding babies".

Malindi said, "It has been planted in our minds that the best person to have privileges is a man. We need to root out that idea. The new government must educate the people. We must discuss violence against women so that we can get rid of it. Men harass their wives. Children get scared. The husband is seen as the lion of the house. They must be tamed. There must be education."

Nomsa said, "Women shall be recognised on merit. There shall be no tokenism. We must be considered for our skills, ability and creativity. Not by sex and gender. The guidelines imply doing away with sexism and racism. It means a declaration of human rights on the home front. We have to decide on the good things of our culture and we must address the outdated and oppressive things. We need to look at the traditional value system that favours men."

Malindi feels that "women must be trained so that we can take up positions in the new government. Men are the ones who oppress us."

145

CODESA

Hundreds of people, Lawyers for Human Rights and the ANC Women's League called on CODESA to do something about the lack of women's involvement in the national negotiations. Women in the different political parties in CODESA agreed there was a problem with the lack of participation of women in CODESA and complained about this to the Management Committee. As a result, a committee was set up to make sure that CODESA's recommendations are non-sexist.

The committee is called the Gender Advisory Committee (GAC). Each of the nineteen parties in CODESA has been asked to send a representative to this committee. The Gender Advisory Committee will look at all the CODESA resolutions to check they are non-sexist. The committee will also advise the different working groups of CODESA on women's problems.

FORCING OPEN THE DOORS – The Women's National Coalition
by Thoraya Pandy

In April 1992, more than 250 women from 60 organisations from all over South Africa joined forces to launch the Women's National Coalition.

"A future non-sexist South Africa depends on us. No one is going to give it to us. We have been banging on doors for generations and nobody has opened them. Now we have to open the doors through the voices of millions of South African women." This was the opening message to the Women's National Coalition launch from Frene Ginwala, deputy head of the ANC's Emancipation Department.

Despite their political differences, women from the ANC, Inkatha, the SACP, the National Party, COSATU and about 55 other organisations agree that women must unite to "force open the doors". They launched the coalition to make sure women's rights are included in the laws and constitution of the new South Africa.

Preparations for the launch began in August after the ANC Women's League called a meeting of different organisations to discuss joint action. Regional coalitions were launched in the Western Cape, the Transvaal and Natal. Other groups are being formed in the Transkei and the Northern Cape. Membership of the coalition is open to individual women and to all organisations which include women.

But how will the coalition make sure women's voices are heard? The meeting decided a Women's Charter must be drawn up and that women must sit on constitution-making committees. "A charter of women's rights must contain what women want – not what lawyers and experts say we need," said Ginwala. "I believe we must grow big ears. We must listen to women everywhere – in rural and urban areas, factory women, women in big mansions, and bring all their demands together."

The meeting set a one-year deadline to draw up the charter. A national steering committee was elected to co-ordinate the process. The committee will also look at how to make sure the charter will really change women's lives.

Beauty Maningi of COSATU said, "We are going to win this struggle. The coalition will not only strengthen our work in COSATU – it will strengthen all women's voices."

Anne Routier of the National Party said, "We have to be tolerant of each other. It is a miracle we have achieved this. But I do feel some things, like the voting, were handled undemocratically." The National Party, together with some other organisations, had wanted all organisations to have the same number of votes. But the meeting decided the organisations with more members would have more votes.

Faith Gasa of Inkatha said, "It is amazing that in two days we were able to sort out very difficult issues. In CODESA very small issues hold us up."

Patricia Dlulane of the ANC Women's League in the Transkei said, "White ladies have always looked down on us, but this forum will prove to them black women are just as capable."

Delegates from the Rural Women's Movement said they would start a village-to-village information campaign about the charter. "We are excited about this. This is the first time rural women have been to such a conference." They were disappointed though that not one "madam" brought her domestic worker to the workshop.

Irene Khumalo of the PAC said bringing women together was a "good thing" but she was tired of white middle-class women dominating meetings.

But despite their differences, delegates were committed to making sure the coalition works.

Delegates at the launch of the Women's National Coalition, April 1992.   *Photo: Anna Zimienski*

Border women look at the law *by Jo Anne Collinge*

Xoliswa Tom is a fieldworker in the Border Council of Churches Development and Training Ministries Programme. She says the Women's Charter Programme is important. It gives women the chance to make their voices heard.

Tom and other women leaders in the Border region believe drawing up the Women's Charter must happen step by step. Educating each other is just as important as drawing up the charter. "The most important thing is empowerment. Women must be able to understand and explain their own situation and to say which needs are most important. Then they must come up with programmes which suit those needs."

Women who cannot read and write are just as capable of taking part as those who have schooling. "Women must stop thinking people are dumb just because they did not go to school," says Tom.

Women have taken seriously that they must understand the law in order to change it. "We first went around to villages asking women to hold meetings to talk about the Women's Charter campaign. At these meetings women elected village representatives for the regional workshop." One-hundred-and-twenty women elected at village level attended the regional workshop on "Women and the Law" in July 1992. Many issues came up.

"There were many things women thought were in the law, but in fact they were just cultural and social issues, just something that has been happening for a long time. Many people did not know where custom stops and the law begins." They were surprised to hear that some of the things which oppress them were not in the law.

Women saw how different marriage laws gave women different rights. "This region is mostly rural, so women are often married under customary law," says Tom. Customary law does not give the wife strong rights. In a region where most women stay in the villages while men go out to work, this can spell trouble. "When the husband stops sending money home and the wife goes to the city to find him, she often finds out he has a second wife. When the first wife tries to fight for her rights the other wife will come up with a marriage certificate. She is more recognised by the law. The rural wife is more recognised by the husbands family," explains Tom.

Tom says the question of customary marriages is closely tied up with the issue of land rights. "Women are working on this land most of the time, because the men are not there. But the men own the land. They can sell the land if they want to." Tom says Border women want to have more discussions about customs which shut women out of decisions about the family. "With migrant labour, a man is only interested in his children when they are old enough to marry. When he sees the girls are all grown up and he knows he will get lobola. The marriage negotiations are between men. Women are not involved. Women say, "These are our children. We are the ones left behind to look after them, to see they get educated."

Women also feel they are denied their proper place when a child dies a violent death. Custom demands men only should be allowed to bury the victims. This is very painful for women. "We want to see where out children are buried," some women said.

Tom says custom is a funny thing. Customs which hold men back are quick to disappear, but customs which oppress women stay firmly in place. "It is one thing for women to become aware of their rights. It is another thing for them to be able to claim these rights in day-to-day living."

Unless women are able to earn their own living, it is very difficult to change customs which keep them from gaining power in the family and in society. This is why in a future South Africa, development programmes (which provide better education, housing and jobs) must pay attention to women, says Tom.

Women at the workshop said women must get special development aid to make up for years and years of being kept from work in the cities. Tom is sure the battle for women's rights will be uphill. In the Ciskei, permission is needed for all meetings of more than 20 people. Already in Jubisa village the headman has refused to allow women to hold a local follow-up meeting to the law workshop. Armed police forced the meeting to disperse when the women tried to go ahead without permission.

Women are deeply affected by the political unrest in the region. Tom says after the recent massacre in Bisho, women were running all over looking for missing children. Including women's rights with human rights is a burning issue for Border women.

Poster: Mannik Design

149

What do women want? *by Glenda Daniels*

The Women's National Coalition is preparing to go out into the field and find out what women want in the "new South Africa". That is what the Women's Charter campaign is all about.

Nenki Matlhare of the Transvaal Rural Women's Movement explains why the Women's Charter campaign is important. "Rural women want to be represented in parliament. We want to be equal to men. We want the power and the right to own our houses. We want the government to legalise our marriages. The husbands of rural women often get married in the cities. If the husband dies, the rural marriage is usually not recognised."

COSATU gender co-ordinator Dorothy Mokgalo says the burning issues for women at work include parental rights, the demand for child-care facilities, an end to sexual harassment and the right to belong to trade unions.

Faith Gasa of the IFP Women's Brigade says IFP women are keen to address domestic and political violence, children's rights, polygamy, divorce laws and the lack of the right to a legal abortion.

The Women's National Coalition launched the charter campaign on 8 March, International Women's Day.

Fieldworkers are being trained and sent to find out about the conditions of women and their demands. Towards the end of the year, booklets and tapes will be made to report back the findings of the research in all languages. After this, regional meetings will be held to adopt the charter. The charter and the recommendations of the conference will be given to the body elected to draw up the constitution for a new South Africa.

Women's voices must be heard in the building of a new constitution.

WOMANDLA – POWER TO WOMEN? At least the Women's Charter gives women a fighting chance

"As women and citizens of South Africa we are here to claim our rights. We want recognition and respect for the work we do in the home, in the workplace and in the community. We want full participation in the creation of a non-sexist, non-racist, democratic South Africa.". These were the words of Frene Ginwala at the launch of the Women's Charter in February 1994.

Three hundred representatives from 92 women's groups around the country adopted the charter at the World Trade Centre. The charter pulls together in a single document the demands, wishes, fears and hopes of women in urban and rural communities, factories, shops and women's meetings.

The charter says, "Women want to control their lives. We bear important responsibilities but lack the authority to make decisions in the home and society. We want shared responsibility and decision-making in the home, and effective equality in politics, the law and in the economy. For too long women have been marginalised, ignored, exploited and are the poorest and most disadvantaged of South Africa. If democracy and human rights are to be meaningful for women they must address our historic subordination and oppression. Women must participate in and shape the nature and form of our democracy."

The charter calls on the state and private companies to provide equal opportunities and equal work for equal pay for women, especially disabled women. The charter says this can be achieved through affirmative action programmes. It states women's unpaid labour (cooking, cleaning, caring for children) should be recognised as contributing to the national wealth and should be included in the country's national accounts.

The charter says there shall be equality within the family, marriage and intimate relationships. That "women married under customary law shall have the right to inherit from their husbands." It calls for shelters and counselling services for the survivors of rape, battery and sexual assault.

It says women must have control over their bodies and the right to choose to have an abortion or not. It calls on the media to change its image of women as sex objects and housewives and to reflect women's contribution in all areas of life.

The charter covers the most crucial demands of women, and it is a victory that women from different political organisations were able to draw up this document. But it has some shortcomings. It is written in a style that is difficult to understand unless one is familiar with all the terms used. Issues such as polygamy, lobola and lesbianism are not dealt with in depth.

The charter will be presented to the Constituent Assembly in June to influence the new constitution and Bill of Rights.

Women in the New South Africa

The following articles consider women's position and role in parliament, in government and the links between women inside and outside parliament.

SPEAK 62, 1994
Women fight on by *Nozizwe Madlala*

The struggle for women's rights is not over yet, warns Nozizwe Madlala, a Member of Parliament in the new government. "Now as never before women must work together and maintain the gains made in the fight for equal rights. It is not good enough just to have women's rights in the constitution. Women have to make sure the laws work for them on a day-to-day basis. Women must be encouraged to claim their rightful place in society.

A special voter in Crossroads, Cape Town, casts her vote with assistance from an Independent Electoral Commission worker.   *Photo: Anna Zimienski*

"Officially the Bill of Rights is more important than customary law. But things will not change overnight. It will be a long road reminding people what their rights and duties are. The new laws will also be given real meaning by challenges in courts. A number of laws which discriminated against women have been scrapped. But, in practice, the situation of women has not changed. For example, although there are equal-pay laws, women in the civil service are still being paid less than men in the same jobs.

"The Women's Charter is a great victory for women but we must still convince our political parties to include it in the new constitution. The transition period gives women a chance to demand change. The election gave women an advantage as all political parties realised the importance of women's votes.

"Women need a strong presence in all areas of government. Women must be encouraged to enter politics and be informed of their rights. Real empowerment means that the culture and style of government has to change to make it more acceptable to women. For women to be effective in rebuilding the new South Africa, men must be prepared to share responsibilities which in the past were seen as women's work. Child care must be provided. Men must do their share of housework. This will allow women to participate fully in nation-building."

SPEAK 62, 1994

Women in power

Our new parliament now has 106 women out of 400 MPs. South Africa has shifted from number 141 on the list of countries with women in parliament to number seven. A woman, Frene Ginwala has been appointed speaker of the new parliament.

When President Nelson Mandela opened parliament he promised women that government would address their needs. "The objectives of the Reconstruction and Development Programme will not have been realised unless we see in practical terms the condition of women in South Africa changing for the better, and that they have the power to intervene in all aspects of life as equals," Mandela said. He also said a gender commission will be appointed and affirmative action programmes would be put in place in all government departments.

However, the upper structures of new government are still male-dominated. There are only two women in the cabinet of 30 ministers – Nkosazana Zuma, Minister of Health, and Stella Sigcau, Minister of Public Enterprises. There are three women deputy ministers – Winnie Mandela (Arts, Culture, Science and Technology), Thoko Msane (Agriculture) and Sanki Nkondo (Welfare and Population Development).

The premiers in all nine regions are men and sixteen of the 90 senators are women.

We spoke to two women ministers, two deputy ministers, a senator and an MP.

Stella Sigcau, Minister of Public Enterprises said, "Economic empowerment of women is a priority. In my department there are very few women on the board of directors and a lot needs to be done to change this. All government and semi-government enterprises are starting affirmative action training programmes. I'm going to make sure there are a fair number of women from both rural and urban areas in these programmes. There will also be marketing and management programmes for women in rural areas. This training will have to go hand-in-hand with providing people with resources to improve their lives, such as electricity and water. Let the burden of women looking for wood be cut. The mistake in the past was to teach women skills without having a market for their products. Women's organisations will play an important role in putting women forward for training."

Nkosazana Zuma said of her appointment as Minister of Health, "At first I was shocked. It was completely unexpected. It is a very big responsibility that rests on my shoulders. But I am excited because the important role women played in the

153

struggle was recognised." Zuma has already made health care free for pregnant women and young children. On Pap smears, which identify cancer of the cervix, Zuma said, "Pap smears will only be taken in high risk cases. Because it is not financially possible, a national screening programme for all women will not take place."

Thoko Msane, Deputy Minister of Agriculture, said her appointment came as a surprise. "When I heard about it I had mixed feelings. On the one hand I felt happy and proud to be representing women; on the other hand, I saw it as a challenge. My appointment should not be seen as an individual thing. If it is to mean anything, women on the ground must get involved. After all, small-scale farmers mainly come from rural areas and most are women. Agriculture is an economic tool to build the economy of the country. Younger women must look at agriculture as a subject to study at tertiary level."

Sanki Nkondo, Deputy Minister of Welfare and Population Development, said, "Claiming child support is not the only problem single mothers face. They have to pay high taxes. This and improving the system of claiming maintenance are areas I consider priorities."

Joyce Kgoali said of her appointment as a senator, "It is challenging. One has to deal with men who seem to be hard-line on women's issues. I am a member of the Rules Committee which sets the code of conduct for the senate. We are only two women out of fifteen on this committee. We end up being watchdogs of women's issues, although men are coming into tune.

"It is important there are women's structures outside parliament to support what is happening inside parliament. Without any support from outside it is pointless. Women parliamentarians must be part of these structures. During breaks in parliament women must go back and account to these structures. As a trade unionist I will not forget about women workers and I will go back to the gender committees in the unions."

Phumzile Ngcuka, Member of Parliament, said, "Women played a central role in bringing the ANC to power. Therefore, more women should have been considered for cabinet positions. It cannot be argued that there is a shortage of women leaders. We believe there is a need for a forum which will make sure the interests of women both inside and outside parliament are considered".

SPEAK 64, 1994
Dynamic Duarte

The PWV's new Minister of Safety and Security, Jessie Duarte, is a woman with a positive outlook on life. She is a rap-loving socialist and calls herself a feminist. She is prepared to rock the boat when it comes to her politics, job and life.

Duarte finds her new job a challenge she could not resist. She grew up in a family where politics was a way of life, and has been a political activist since she was a teenager. "My grandmother was a socialist in her beliefs and actions. She had the most influence on me as a child and through my teenage years. I started out being active in the residents' association in Newclare, Johannesburg, where I grew up."

In 1982 Duarte was elected secretary of the Federation of Transvaal Women and was twice elected its representative in the United Democratic Front.

"I believe there is a need for women to be organised separately. When I was a women's representative on the UDF, somehow the voice of women was organised and heard in that forum." Duarte believes the Women's National Coalition has failed to build a national women's movement although it tried.

"Unfortunately the coalition tended to raise more issues of the middle class instead of issues affecting working, unemployed and women who are not organised. They did have a vision. I applaud that. If it was not for the coalition we would not have clauses in the constitution recognising the special problems of women."

On being a mother, Duarte said, "I don't like it when women's role as mothers is overemphasised. However, the reality is that I still have these tasks. Even though I am Provincial Minister for Safety and Security I still have to make sure my family is taken care of. As a woman I have to fight a struggle in a male-dominated world. I feel I have achieved a situation in my family where we all share the tasks."

On men, she said, "We have educated men on the language of gender equality but we haven't actually educated them on the reality of gender equality."

Duarte is keen to work with other women in parliament to make sure equality becomes a reality. "I would like to see women in parliament raising issues from a women's perspective. I see myself raising the profile of women in the police force."

Duarte has to deal with crime as a matter of urgency. Another issue that concerns her is domestic violence. "The police have to learn that abuse of any person is abuse. If a person reports that as a crime, they need to arrest and charge the person." Women and communities also need to act. "A lot of abuse is seen as part and parcel of a good marriage," she said. "I've heard comments like 'If my husband does not beat me it means he does not love me.' Women have to recognise they have rights and they have to learn to use those rights. The issue has to be taken up by the community. If you hear a neighbour being beaten up you must try to help."

On rape, Duarte said, "There's nothing at the moment that makes a woman feel safe anywhere. One way we can develop better security for women is more education on how to protect themselves. The number of rapes in the family is on the increase, and it is happening to very young children. I read a story where a young girl was raped and when the man was convicted the family blamed the girl because the rapist was the breadwinner."

According to police statistics, 221 children, including toddlers, were raped in Soweto since the beginning of the year. "We need to take a well-run education programme to schools, factories, television and radio. Many people, even women, do not have an understanding of the tragedy of rape. I've heard women say 'It's her fault because of the way she was dressed', 'She asked for it' or 'She seduced the man.' Rape is contributing to the spread of HIV and AIDS.

Duarte believes society must be liberated to accept the rights of gays and lesbians. She also feels a woman should have the right to control over her own body.

Asked for her views on prostitution, Duarte said, "Prostitution is the way some women make a living. We have to find a way to make it healthy and safe. We have to protect women from being exploited by pimps and police who buy their services or get them as favours for not making arrests. I would want to see some age limit. The present legal age in countries where prostitution is legal is eighteen. We need to work towards a situation where we can perhaps suggest it be legalised."

SPEAK 66, 1994
Affirmative action

"We need affirmative action," say many people, "if we are really going to build a new South Africa." Hearing this usually sends shivers of fear down the spines of those who benefited in the old South Africa.

It gives rays of hope, however, to black people and women, that they may at last get some decent opportunities.

SPEAK 67, 1994
Should the sisters do it for themselves? *by Rosalee Telela*

"Women cannot pin their hopes on what women in parliament could achieve for them. Women do not even form half of parliament and their hands are tied by the parties they belong to."

That's the view of Debbie Bonnin of the Agenda collective which publishes a journal about women and gender. She firmly believes: "We should form a national independent movement which will put the interests of women first, as opposed to the interests of political parties, churches, unions or civics." Those who agree with Bonnin argue that such issues as polygamy, abortion, violence against women and equality in the home won't come to the top of the agenda in broad organisations or in women's groups which are part of broader organisations. What they want is an organisation run by women and focused on women's needs.

Asha Moodley, Head of AZAPO's Secretariat for Information and Research, said, "Women need an independent movement for direction. We need to grab power in our hands so we can define our own agendas and policies and not just slot into political parties."

Daphne Mashile-Nkosi of the Rural Women's Movement said, "Political Parties can raise the issues in parliament. Women need a platform where it will be easy for them to raise their issues."

But do women from different backgrounds have so much in common? Bonnin agrees it will not be easy to bring everyone together. "Women are divided by race, class, urban and rural experience, religion, language, culture. These differences could limit what an independent women's movement can achieve. Take the issue of abortion: some women might want it legalised, others, say from a church group, might take a different stand." However, Bonnin agrees that some issues will unite women. "If we had such a movement today we'd be able to challenge the growing pornography industry in this country. The few people challenging it only speak from a conservative viewpoint. Nobody is taking the line that pornography oppresses all women."

Ntombi Shope of the ANC Women's League said divisions between women can be overcome in a movement. "Things like race and class will not matter, because the movement will be looking at the problems of all women. Coming together will help women understand each other. It will break down walls between black and white, urban and rural, working and middle classes." Shope sees an independent movement as allowing women "to make decisions for themselves without worrying about what their organisations or parties will say".

The Women's National Coalition was one women's organisation that brought together women from various political parties and other organisations to lobby women's interests at the multi-party talks. Bonnin said of the WNC, "It was dominated by political parties. Because of its nature, issues such as abortion were never resolved."

Moodley said, "The majority of women never heard of it or the Women's Charter it drew up."

Annemarie Nutt, national executive member of the WNC, suggested reasons for this. The WNC organised in a top-down way, taking on too much of the character of the political parties which dominated it. Nutt feels that a new movement is needed. "Unlike the WNC, this new movement will need to be politically independent and to organise from the bottom up."

Struggles Today

In the articles that follow, women in the Western Cape speak of making the idea of an independent women's movement real; women in one of the provincial legislatures speak of their experiences and difficulties; and the director of the Women's National Coalition shares her thoughts on the challenges facing women in the new South Africa. These interviews were conducted during 1996 and 1997.

The New Women's Movement

One group of women who have acted on setting up a politically independent organisation is the New Women's Movement (NWM). Interviewed in 1997, Vainola Makan and Laurie Watson of NWM said that the idea of an independent women's movement had been under discussion for a long time in the Western Cape. They began to make this idea a reality in 1996.

Individuals involved in the Women's National Coalition felt that an independent grassroots women's movement, free of the pressures of party politics, was an important vehicle to take the needs of grassroots women forward. Especially during the present period of transition. Makan and Watson point out that party political organisations such as the ANC Women's League are restricted because it is "located within the present government. Questions we raise are: Are they independent and autonomous? Can they raise questions to do with ANC policy?"

The NWM is independent. It is not, says Makan, "an appendage to a broader organisation". A link between the NWM and the WNC exists, with members of the NWM attending the annual general meeting of the WNC.

Watson says: "We are non-party political but not apolitical. We stand for poor, grassroots, marginalised women. We take up issues such as poverty. We campaign around issues such as the cost of living or child maintenance. We are accountable and democratic. We have delayed selecting people in leadership. In all areas representatives are being elected. We are waiting for the launch".

They are going this route as they want to avoid the power struggles they see often occurring in women's organisations.

Makan points out: "We have an interim steering committee of about 20 women from all areas – Cape Town, Stellenbosch, Ceres. This includes urban, peri-urban and rural areas. Many of us in urban areas organise rural women. We want them to join us."

One of the many challenges of the NWM is to bring women together across racial divides. The NWM stands for anti-racism, anti-bias. It tries to break down racial prejudices. "We have done a lot as a young movement," says Makan. "People from Mitchell's Plain, Langa, Guguletu are in the movement." The NWM believes that if differences are not acknowledged and worked with this will prevent the building of a strong women's movement. "Racism is the history of apartheid. All of us – African, Indian, coloured – have internalised racist attitudes. This is not institutionalised power. It is not the same as racism."

The vision is to build a strong and independent grassroots movement that will unite women across colour and urban-rural divides around issues that affect marginalised, disadvantaged women in impoverished conditions. "The state will never have the capacity to do that. If you look at the nature of the state, it looks at middle-class interests and concerns. We are looking deeper than that," says Makan.

The government, they point out, has put in place a lot of national machinery for addressing gender equity. But the commitment is not translated into action. It is hampered by a top-down approach and by budgetary constraints.

The nature of the institution of government has lots of constraints, they say. "There are many women in parliament but they are not there because they represent women. They represent their parties. If we want to get them to take women's issues

158

WOMEN: WE FOUGHT FOR THE VOTE

WOMEN ARE LEADERS!

WOMEN MUST OWN THE LAND AS WELL AS WORK ON IT

I am a woman – not a Toy!

NO TO VIOLENCE ABUSE AND SEXUAL HARASSMENT – WE HAVE A RIGHT TO CONTROL OUR BODIES

EQUAL PAY FOR EQUAL WORK

WOMEN AND MEN MUST SHARE WORK IN THE FAMILY

NOW WE MUST CLAIM OUR RIGHTS!

Poster: Judy Seidman

up in parliament we need to hold them accountable. We need a strong women's movement to keep women accountable – strong civil society is needed.

"The changes we have seen are changes in the colour and gender of who is in the state. And the gender machinery makes people feel things will be attended to."

Watson and Makan point out that during this period of transition, a process of de-mobilisation has taken place, with the disbanding of many organisations of the past. They also see a climate of apathy. They are trying to mobilise, in this context, around cost-of-living issues such as the prices of milk, bread and paraffin. They are demanding no increases and no VAT on basic foods. "The lives of ordinary people have not changed," they say.

Together with other Western Cape groups, the NWM launched a campaign in early 1997 against a Department of Welfare proposal that threatened to reduce child maintenance grants. These grants were available under apartheid policy to children under eighteen within families whose incomes were below the poverty line, in white, coloured and Indian communities. In order to make such grants available to African South Africans, the Department of Welfare was proposing to stretch limited funds by reducing the amount of the grant and reducing the eligibility to children under ten.

Makan points out: "Women affected were not informed. The NWM called meetings to inform women. Over four weeks we held meetings in 20 areas to tell women. In every area women said, we want to take action. For the first time since the 1980s women wanted to take to the streets. Women stood up saying, 'I will have to take my child out of school.' There was a big response. Sometimes as many as 200 people attended meetings. Our demand is that the parent allowance should not be scrapped. That there should be no cuts in maintenance, and no drop in the age. That the budget be re-prioritised to redress past imbalances and to redistribute. Government needs to look at other areas where they can cut. Instead of taxing the rich, government is taxing the poor. They should cut the military budget instead. The state is moving away from social spending. We need to relook at government's macro-economic policy. We will simultaneously be involved in lobbying and advocacy, and organising at grassroots level."

Women in parliament and the country – Making links

We spoke to Loretta Jacobus of the Gauteng parliament. During the 1980s, Loretta was a community activist in Riverlea, outside Johannesburg, and an executive member of the UDF-aligned Federation of Transvaal Women during the 1980s. After the unbannings of political organisations in 1990, Loretta was active in the ANC branch in her area and was the chairperson of the SACP Johannesburg branch.

Loretta points to the gain women made in getting the ANC to agree that women should constitute at least one third of the lists to parliament. "We fought together and made decisions together. Twenty-five percent of the legislature are now women."

Loretta's responsibilities as a member of the provincial legislature includes serving on standing committees for social welfare and health, and she is the convenor of the gender sub-committee set up within the petitions and public participation committee. In addition she has ANC constituency work in Alexandra township. Loretta says, "The workload is heavy. You have to do constituency work. You have to attend meetings at all hours. You have no time to socialise. People don't know what you are doing and organisations feel you have abandoned them. They then isolate you."

Loretta feels this is unfair as "they elected us; they cannot now leave us to swim. Communication is a two way process." She tries to keep in touch with women's organisations and the main way this happens is when she gets asked to speak at events. However, organisations that placed the women in provincial and national parliaments are not as strong as they used to be.

"Women's organisation is degenerating – they were strong as a broad movement. During the pre-negotiation years there was collective organisation, a commitment and closeness in organisations such as FEDTRAW. There was one common goal, one common enemy."

The problem today also lies partly in not being clear about parliament and about who to put in parliament, says Loretta. "We pushed everyone into parliament. People did not know what parliament was. And we did not develop other women. So today the majority of the women leaders are in parliament, and not in organisations such as the Women's League." For the forthcoming elections, says Loretta, "we need to think about where to place people".

Both men and women in parliament have had problems coping with their new tasks. Most did not realise what the life of an MP would mean. Loretta says that there were "lots of problems with no real difference between men and women in parliament" in some respects. Overall, however, women in parliament are at a greater disadvantage than men. Men tend to be more skilled and have more academic qualifications than the women in parliament. Men are also encouraged more than women to study. "Not much has been done to empower women," says Loretta. "One women has just spoken once – she was so scared. And she felt disempowered because she made blunders and people laughed."

Members of the legislature also pay the price of relationships and marriages falling apart. Often this is worse for women as their high-powered positions threaten their men, who are not in positions of equal power.

Loretta herself seems to be managing to swim her way through her job. What was it in her previous experience that helped her in parliament today? Without a moment's hesitation Loretta says,"It was my experience in the Party (SACP). I was thrown in at the deep end when I was made chair of the SACP Johannesburg branch. I was petrified at my first meeting after being elected chairperson. I hoped no one would come to this meeting. Before the meeting started I said to the comrades, 'You must help me. I don't know how to do this. If you laugh at my mistakes you will show yourselves to be more stupid than me.' They supported me. I learnt. I accepted the challenge and developed myself."

Loretta developed further during the multi-party negotiations when, in response to the call by women for equal participation in the negotiations, each party agreed to have two delegates – one woman and one man. But as Loretta points out, being on these teams was not empowering for all women. She was empowered, she says, because of the support she got from her partner in the SACP negotiating team – Joe Slovo.

"Joe Slovo really empowered me. He said, 'No one will laugh at you. Ask whatever you want, make whatever input you want'. He had so much confidence in me. My experience was very different from the woman in the next delegation. She had to consult her male partner even before she could ask a question. Once she asked a question when the male delegate was out of the room. When he got back he shouted at her and she was in tears. This woman was disempowered. The man was even younger than her."

Loretta's experience as a community activist and as a trained social worker also helps her in the work she does in the provincial legislature today. The issues she has to deal with on the health and welfare committees is not too different from issues she dealt with when working in her community.

Loretta says the major problems of women in South Africa today are abuse, harassment and violence in the home and the workplace. She sees both government and community organisations as having a role to play in these problems. "Community organisations can play a role in monitoring how government deals with these problems. Government can play a role in educating women on their rights, how to demand their rights, so they don't take the abuse. We need to keep the constitution alive, to make it work for us."

What does Loretta feel has been achieved in parliament to date? "In terms of what we thought we would be able to do, our expectations have not been met," she says. "People need to understand the bureaucracy, the wheels of government, the procedures. Things don't happen overnight. Things move very slowly, so people feel disillusioned".

Loretta admits that compromises have had to be made within the legislature. "Politicians make compromises in the interests of the province. We know what we experienced. We have lived the hardship of not having a home. But we have to look at the realities of the matter. We have to make laws that will govern the province of 6,5 million people and not lead to chaos. Our constituency as a legislature is not only an ANC constituency."

Loretta does not regret her decision to go into the provincial legislature. "I don't regret it. I have my down moments, but the bottom line is, I feel I have made a contribution in whatever minor way".

We also interviewed Maggie Magubane and Rafilwe Ndzuta, Members of the Gauteng Provincial Legislature. They maintain contact with the trade unions which sent them to parliament only when invited by those organisations. They are sometimes invited and at times still play a role in the unions they came from. Maggie says, "I attended the COSATU Women's Congress in May 1996."

Rafilwe says, "I am in touch with the Wits branch. They call on me to boost the morale of women and to attend meetings. I was invited as the keynote speaker at the Wits AGM of the Paper, Pulp, Wood and Allied Workers' Union. It was wonderful. The new comrades told me, 'You have clarified things for us – we understand better now.'"

The unions have changed since these and other comrades went into parliament. Besides losing key leaders, the unions have had to make changes as a result of the changing political scene. Keeping in touch with the comrades they put in parliament is not an easy matter, and unions do not seem to have developed ways of doing this.

From the side of the women trade unionists now in parliament, it is an equally difficult matter. Besides the workload, being in a provincial parliament means learning new approaches. Labour is not a provincial matter but is addressed by the national parliament. This means that there is no provincial structure for labour matters.

Maggie and Rafilwe therefore sit on committees covering matters that are new to them. They have to teach themselves the business of these committees as they go along. Maggie sits on the following committees: health, agriculture/conservation, internal arrangements and economic affairs/ finance. Rafilwe sits on the committees on health, sports/arts/culture, social welfare, public accounts and petitions and public participation, and is an alternate in internal arrangements.

They find this very challenging and both agree that they are amazed at how fast they have learnt. They keep in touch with what is happening on the ground through their ANC branches. Although ANC branches are weak, they are continuing to meet.

The Women's National Coalition

In an interview in March 1997, Mahau Phekoe of the Women's National Coalition said that we needed to draw on our history of struggle to advance women's struggles today. "We need to harness that energy again. In the past we had debates on national or women's liberation. Many said these would go hand-in-hand. We spent a lot of time harnessing national liberation. But the struggle for women is just beginning.

"The coalition is looking at a number of processes. Structural changes are taking place in the coalition. The country is transforming – the oalition has to transform as well."

The coalition's major project was the Women's Charter, launched in 1994. The process leading to the charter was participatory. But, as Mahau points out, collating women's demands took time and it was a while before the coalition got back to the women. Affiliated organisations in the meanwhile "went their own way, and set their own priorities. The coalition did not provide leadership. As people moved into parliament the picture changed. There was a leadership vacuum."

Today, says Mahau, "Human capacity is an extreme problem. It is difficult to find African women for jobs in NGOs. What is the answer? Do you hire white women and organise mentoring? This is a frustrating capacity problem in NGOs."

Mahau points out that the "vacuum in leadership is very real in civil society as a whole. We need representation of women in large numbers in all tiers of government – at present we don't have enough at local government. We need to train women for government and civil society."

Often women MPs cannot cope with the demands of parliament, says Mahau. "At the last budget speech, three women commented on the budget. One read a speech written in English. She struggled with what she had to say. No one heard what she said. Comments were made on her bad delivery. The other two had done no research. This discredited these women.

"We need to build the capacity of women in parliament – so they can speak in an informed way. We also need gender training for women and men. Women have the responsibility to train other women on the outside on what it means to be a candidate, how government works, how we can build an alternative to present government structures. We are in the old masters' seats, we have not changed this. We need to look at how we can restructure. We need to change the language used, the procedure, the protocols.

"Before the next national and local elections we need to run training sessions on what it means to be a candidate. We did not necessarily get the best women representatives (in 1994). Women did not know what to expect. In civil society we need to network more, talk to each other, know who is available, committed, and able to build. We need to ask who can we sacrifice on the inside.

"In our latest strategic plan, the WNC has come up with a mission to promote gender equality to improve the lives of South Africans as a whole. Building on WNC strengths, we are building networks of women. Not an umbrella as an umbrella structure seems to impose on women."

The WNC will focus on lobbying (of government), training (for parliamentary and local government candidates, community leaders and in adult basic education) and gender training.

WOMEN OF AFRICA – Sma Khubeka

We women of Africa
have suffered so much
In the hands of the law
Being taken as inferiors
Being deprived of our rights
At work and at home
    We say
No matter how long the distance can be
No matter how slippery the road can be
No matter how high the mountain can be
We won't go back
We will move forward
Until we reach our destiny
So,
Let's join hands and move forward
And say
FREEDOM NOW!

Graphic: SPEAK

Abbreviations

ADAPT – Agisanang Domestic Abuse Prevention and Training
ANC – African National Congress
ANCWL – African National Congress Women's League
ARAG – Abortion Reform Action Group
AWO – African Women's Organisation
AZAPO – Azanian People's Organisation

CCB – Civil Co–operation Bureau
CCAWUSA – Commercial, Catering and Allied Workers' Union
CEC – Central Executive Council
CODESA – Convention for a Democratic South Africa

FEDTRAW – Federation of Transvaal Women
FOSATU – Federation of South African Trade Unions

GAC – Gender Advisory Committee
GASEWU – Gauteng Self–Employed Women's Union
GLOW – Gay and Lesbian Organisation of the Witwatersrand

IBA – Independent Broadcasting Authority
IFP – Inkatha Freedom Party
ISU – Internal Stability Unit

MAAWU – Metal and Allied Workers' Union
MDM – Mass Democratic Movement
MEC – Member of the Executive Committee
MHF – Moutse Health Forum
MK – Umkhonto we Sizwe

NEC – National Executive Committee
NEDLAC – National Economic Development and Labour Council
NEHAWU – National Education and Health Workers' Union

NGO – Non-government Organisation
NOW – Natal Organisation of Women
NPPHC – National Progressive Primary Health Care Network
NUMSA – National Union of Metal Workers of South Africa
NWM – New Women's Movement

PAC – Pan African Congress
PAWO – Port Alfred Women's Organisation
POWA – People Opposed to Women Abuse
PPWAWU – Paper, Pulp, Wood and Allied Workers' Union
PWV – Pretoria–Witwatersrand–Vereeniging

RAP – Radio Audio Programme
RWM – Rural Women's Movement

SACCAWU – South African Commercial, Catering and Allied Workers' Union
SACP – South African Communist Party
SADF – South African Defence Force
SADWU – South African Domestic Workers' Union
SARHWU – South African Railways and Harbour Workers' Union
SEWU – Self–Employed Women's Union

TGWU – Transport and General Workers' Union
TRAC – Transvaal Rural Action Committee

UDF – United Democratic Front
UWCO – United Women's Congress

WILDD – Women's Institute for Leadership, Democracy and Development
WNC – Women's National Coalition
WOSA – Workers' Organisation for Socialist Action